I0119524

D. W Miller

Sabbath Songs and Spiritual Songs

D. W Miller

Sabbath Songs and Spiritual Songs

ISBN/EAN: 9783337334857

Printed in Europe, USA, Canada, Australia, Japan

Cover: Foto ©Thomas Meinert / pixelio.de

More available books at **www.hansebooks.com**

SABBATH SONGS

AND

SPIRITUAL HYMNS

FOR

Sabbath Schools,

GOSPEL MEETINGS AND THE HOME CIRCLE:

BY

D. W. MILLER.

———◦)◦═◈═◦(◦———

CINCINNATI:

PUBLISHED BY D. W. MILLER.

1881.

SABBATH SONGS

AND

SPIRITUAL HYMNS.

SILVER STREET. S. M.

I. SMITH.

Come, sound His praise a - broad, And hymns of glo - ry sing;

Je - ho - vah is the sov' - reign God, The u - ni - ver - sal King.

1 Come, sound His praise abroad,
And hymns of glory sing;
Jehovah is the sovereign God,
The universal King.

2 He formed the deeps unknown;
He gave the seas their bound;
The watery worlds are all His own,
And all the solid ground.

3 Come, worship at His throne,
Come, bow before the Lord;
We are His works, and not our own,
He formed us by His word.

4 To-day attend His voice,
Nor dare provoke His rod;
Come, like the people of His choice,
And own your gracious God.

5 But if your ears refuse
The language of His grace, [Jews,
And hearts grow hard, like stubborn
That unbelieving race:

6 The Lord, in vengeance drest,
Will lift His hand and swear,
"You that despise my promised rest
Shall have no portion there."

1 Grace! 'tis a charming sound,
Harmonious to mine ear:
Heaven with the echo shall resound,
And all the earth shall hear.

2 Grace first contrived the way
To save rebellious man;
And all the steps that grace display,
Which drew the wondrous plan.

3 Grace first inscribed my name
In God's eternal book;
'Twas grace that gave me to the Lamb,
Who all my sorrows took.

4 Grace led my roving feet
To tread that heavenly road;
And new supplies each hour I meet
While pressing on to God.

5 Grace taught my soul to pray,
And made my eyes o'erflow:
'Twas grace that kept me to this day,
And will not let me go.

6 Grace all the work shall crown,
Through everlasting days;
It lays in heaven the topmost stone,
And well deserves the praise. (3)

GLORY IN THE CROSS.

God forbid that I should glory save in the cross of our Lord Jesus Christ.—Gal. vi: 14.

D. W. MILLER.   D. W. MILLER.

1. In the cross of Christ I'll glo - ry, And I long to tell the sto - ry
2. Like the rainbow's radiant glory, Like the mountain's summit hoary
3. Now the ha-lo of the glo - ry Circling round the ancient sto - ry

How he died for me; And on Calv'ry's sacred mountain Of-fered
In the sun's bright rays; Stands the cross, his love as-sur-ing, Firm, im-
Breaks to bright-est day; And its rays with growing splendor Rend the

REFRAIN.

there himself a ran-som, That I might be free.
mu - table, en-dur - ing, Till the end-less days. In the cross of Christ I'll
dark'ning vail asun-der, 'Twixt my God and me.

glory, And I'll tell the wondrous sto - ry Of his love for me; For with

precious blood he bought me, And with love unchanging sought me, That I his might be.

ARCHANGEL.

D. W. Miller.   *Psalm 148.*   D. W. Miller.

1. Praise ye the Lord! From the heav-ens sound his praise on high;
2. Oh, heav'ns give praise! And ye floods on high, all praise his name;

Praise him ye an - gel - hosts to him so nigh.
His law, de - creed, shall ev - er be the same.

Praise him ye sun and moon, Stars of light And worlds unknown;
O earth, your ter - rors bring, Fire, hail, snow, And wind shall sing,

Praise him whose might made all things at his word.
His word they know, to him their song they raise.

3 Oh, praise his name!
Hills and mountains, and all living things,
Praise him ye people, and ye earth-born kings,
Princes and judges, all,
Old and young,
Before him fall,
Let every tongue
Forever sound his fame.

4 Praise him ye host!
Men and angels, earth, and heav'n above,
Oh, praise his name, his glory, power, and love.
Let all his praise proclaim,
Glorify
His holy name,
Father on high,
Blest Son, and Holy Ghost.

ONWARD CHRISTIAN SOLDIERS.

Rev. S. BARING GOULD. JOS. F. HAYDN, arr. by D. W. MILLER.

1. On-ward, Christian sol - diers, Marching to the war, With the cross of
2. At the sign of tri - umph, Satan's hosts do flee; On, then, Christian
3. Like a might-y ar - my Moves the church of God; Brothers, we are

Je - sus Go - ing on be - fore; Christ, the Royal Mas-ter, Leads a-gain the
sol - diers, On to vic-to - ry! Hell's foundations quiver, At the shout of
treading Where the saints have trod. We are not di-vid - ed, All one body

CHORUS.

foe; For-ward in - to bat - tle, See, His banner go.
praise; Brothers, lift your voices, Loud your anthems raise. Onward, Christian
we; One in hope and doctrine, One in char-i - ty.

soldiers, Marching to the war, With the cross of Jesus Go-ing on be-fore.

4 Crowns and thorns may perish,
   Kingdoms rise and wane;
But the church of Jesus
   Constant will remain.
Gates of hell can never
   'Gainst that church prevail;
We have Christ's own promise,
   And that can not fail.

5 Onward, then, ye people,
   Join the happy throng;
Blend with ours your voices
   In triumphant song.
Glory, praise, and honor,
   Unto Christ, the King;
This through countless ages,
   Men and angels sing.

JESUS, MY SAVIOR.

D. W. MILLER.   *My Lord and my God.*—Jno. xx: 28.   D. W. MILLER.

1. Je - sus, my Sav-iour, my Lov-er, and Friend, Now I con-
2. Rays of bright sun-shine now beam from thy face, Fil - ling my

fess thee, and hum-bly I bend; All earth's vain pleasures I
soul with thy sweet ho - ly grace; Heav-en - ly mu - sic has

count meanest dross, Rest-ing in peace at the foot of the cross.
ravished mine ear, Mu - sic of Je - sus' name ev - er so dear.

CHORUS.

Jesus, my Saviour, To thee I'll sing, Glory for-ev - er, Jesus, my King.

3 Thou'lt not forsake me: thy love has no end;
Keep me so faithful, I'll ne'er thee offend;
But if temptation should lead me astray,
Gently, Lord, lead me in thy loving way. *Cho.*

4 Ne'er will I sorrow, rejoicing alway;
Jesus my song is by night and by day;
Soon will I rise to my treasure above,
Ever to sing and to live in his love. *Cho.*

WESTWOOD. 8s & 7s.

D. W. MILLER.

Sav - iour, breathe an eve - ning bless - ing, Ere re-

pose our spir - its seal; Sin and want we come con-

fess - ing, Thou canst save, and Thou canst heal.

1 Saviour, breathe an evening blessing,
  Ere repose our spirits seal;
Sin and want we come confessing,
  Thou canst save, and Thou canst heal.

2 Though the night be dark and dreary,
  Darkness can not hide from Thee;
Thou art He who, never weary,
  Watchest where Thy people be.

3 Though destruction walk around us,
  Though the arrows past us fly,
Angel guards from Thee surround us;
  We are safe if Thou art nigh.

4 Should swift death this night o'ertake us,
  And command us to the tomb, [us,
May the morn in heaven awake us,
  Clad in light and fadeless bloom.

1 We are watching, we are waiting
  For the bright prophetic day,
When the shadows, weary shadows,
  From the world shall roll away.

2 We are watching, we are waiting
  For the star that brings the day
When the night of sin shall vanish,
  And the shadows melt away.

3 We are watching, we are waiting
  For the beauteous King of day,
For the chiefest of ten thousand,
  For the Light, the Truth, the Way.

4 We are watching, we are waiting
  For the dawn of heavenly light,
For the coming of the Kingdom,
  Day that ne'er shall know the night.

1. A-wake, my soul, in joy-ful lays, And sing Thy great Re-
2. He saw me ru-ined in the fall, Yet loved me not-with-

deem-er's praise; He just-ly claims a song from me: His
stand-ing all; He saved me from my lost es-tate: His

lov-ing kind-ness, oh, how free! His lov-ing kindness,
lov-ing kind-ness, oh, how great! His lov-ing kindness,

lov-ing kind-ness, His lov-ing kind-ness, oh, how free.
lov-ing kind-ness, His lov-ing kind-ness, oh, how great.

3 When trouble, like a gloomy cloud,
Has gathered thick and thundered loud,
He near my soul has always stood:
His loving kindness, oh, how good!

4 Often I feel my sinful heart
Prone from my Jesus to depart;
But though I have Him oft forgot,
His loving kindness changes not.

5 Soon shall I pass the gloomy vale,
Soon all my mortal powers must fail;
Oh, may my last expiring breath
His loving kindness sing in death.

6 Then let me mount and soar away
To those bright worlds of endless day,
And sing with rapture and surprise
His loving kindness in the skies.

JESUS CALLS.

Who is even at the right hand of God: who also maketh intercession for us.—Rom. viii : 34.

D. W. MILLER.   D. W. MILLER.

1. Come, Je - sus now calls to thee; Come, for - giveness is free;

Come, taste of the Saviour's love; Je - sus calls from a - bove.

REFRAIN.

Weep - ing in Gethsem - a - ne, Bleed - ing, dy - ing, on the tree;

Plead he once in ag - o - ny; Now he calls from a - bove.

Come unto me all ye that labor and are heavy laden, and I will give you rest.—Matt. xi : 31.

2 Come, lean on the Saviour's breast;
Come, poor sinner, find rest;
Come, see like a wooing dove;
Jesus calls from above. *Ref.*

He that cometh unto me I will in no wise cast out.—Jno. vi : 37.

3 Come, hear now the Saviour's voice;
Come, believe and rejoice;
Come, wand'rer, no longer rove,
Jesus calls from above. *Ref.*

Neither is there salvation in any other.—Acts iv : 12.

4 Come, he is the only way;
Come, your sins on him lay;
Come, broken hearts he will love;
Jesus calls from above. *Ref.*

D. W. MILLER.

1. Am I called? and can it be? Has my Sav - iour
cho - sen me? Guilt - y, wretch - ed as I am,
Has he named my worth - less name? Vi - lest of the
vile am I, Dare I raise my hopes so high?

2 Am I called? I dare not stay,
May not, must not disobey;
Here I lay me at thy feet,
Clinging to the mercy-seat!
Thine I am, and thine alone,
Lord with me thy will be done.

3 Am I called? an heir of God?
Washed, redeemed by precious blood?
Father, lead me by thy hand,
Guide me to that better land,
Where my soul shall be at rest,
Pillowed on my Saviour's breast.

JESUS, THY NAME I LOVE.

D. W. MILLER.

1. Je - sus! Thy name I love All oth - er
2. Thou bless - ed Son of God! Hast bought me

names a - bove, Je - sus, my Lord; O Thou art
with Thy blood, Je - sus, my Lord; Oh, how great

all to me; Noth - ing to please I see,
is Thy love All oth - er loves a - bove,

Noth - ing a - part from Thee, Je - sus, my Lord!
Love that I dai - ly prove, Je - sus, my Lord!

3 When unto Thee I flee,
Thou wilt my refuge be,
  Jesus, my Lord!
What need I now to fear?
What earthly grief or care,
Since Thou art ever near?
  Jesus, my Lord!

4 Soon Thou wilt come again,
I shall be happy then,
  Jesus, my Lord?
Then Thine own face I'll see,
Then I shall like Thee be,
Be evermore with Thee,
  Jesus, my Lord!

Thou Lord art our Father, our Redeemer.—Isa. lxiii: 16.

D. W. MILLER. D. W. MILLER.

1. From the glorious heav-en Where the an-gels are, God our heavenly Fa-ther, Se-eth us a-far. Hear-eth all we ask for, Ev-ery night and day, And in ten-der mer-cy O'er our work and play Broods in lov-ing kind-ness, Lest we go a-stray.

2 As a father giveth,
   So he gives us bread,
Saves us out of danger,
   Watches by our bed.
In our joy or sorrow,
   He is ever near,
Covered by his wings of love,
   We need have no fear,
Through the darkest trials
   Shines his promise clear.

3 For he loves and pities
   All his children so,
That his Son to save us,
   Came to earth below.
If you'll fully trust him,
   He will cleanse your sin,
And at last the Father
   Heavenly gates within,
Will with loving welcome
   Bid us enter in.

ABOVE ALL OTHERS.

D. W. MILLER.

1. One there is a-bove all oth-ers, Well deserves the name of Friend;
2. When He lived on earth a-bas-ed, Friend of sin-ners was His name;

His is love be-yond a broth-er's, Cost-ly, free, and knows no end.
Now a-bove all glo-ry rais-ed, He re-joic-es in the same.

Which of all our friends to save us, Could or would have shed his blood,
Oh, for grace our hearts to soft-en, Teach us, Lord, at length to love,

But this Sav-ior died to have us Rec-on-ciled in Him to God.
We a-las! for-get too oft-en, What a Friend we have a-bove.

1. Just as I am, without one plea, But that Thy blood was shed for me,

And that Thou bidst me come to Thee, O Lamb of God, I come, I come.

2 Just as I am, and waiting not,
To rid myself of one dark blot, [spot,
To Thee, whose blood can cleanse each
    O Lamb of God, I come! I come!

3 Just as I am, though tossed about,
With many a conflict, many a doubt,
Fightings within, and fears without,
    O Lamb of God, I come! I come!

4 Just as I am, poor, wretched, blind;
Sight, riches, healing of the mind,
Yes, all I need, in Thee I find,
    O Lamb of God, I come! I come!

5 Just as I am, Thou wilt receive,
Wilt welcome, pardon, cleanse, relieve,
Because Thy promise I believe,
    O Lamb of God, I come! I come!

6 Just as I am, Thy love unknown,
Hath broken every barrier down;
Now to be Thine, yea, Thine alone,
    O Lamb of God, I come! I come!

HEBRON. KEY B♭.
1 Thus far the Lord hath led me on;
Thus far His power prolongs my days;
And every evening shall make known
Some fresh memorial of His grace.

2 Much of my time has run to waste,
And I, perhaps, am near my home;
But He forgives my follies past.[come.
And gives me strength for days to

REST. KEY E♭.
1 Asleep in Jesus! blessed sleep!
From which none ever wake to weep;
A calm and undisturbed repose,
Unbroken by the last of foes.

2 Asleep in Jesus! oh how sweet
To be for such a slumber meet!
With holy confidence to sing
That death hath lost its venomed sting!

3 Asleep in Jesus! oh, for me
May such a blissful refuge be:
Securely shall my ashes lie,
And wait the summons from on high.

THE IMPORTUNATE SINNER.

D. W. MILLER.

Gently.

1. Lord, I can not let Thee go   Till a blessing Thou be - stow;
2. Thou hast helped in ev - 'ry need;   This em-bold-ens me to   plead;

Do not turn a - way Thy face,   Mine's an ur-gent, pressing   case.
Af - ter so much mer - cy past,   Canst Thou let me sink at   last?

Once a sin-ner near de - spair   Sought Thy mer-cy-seat   in prayer;
No, I must maintain my   hold,   'Tis Thy goodness makes me bold;

Mercy heard, and set him free;   Lord, that mer-cy came to   me.
I can no de - ni - al   take   When I plead for Je - sus' sake.

1 Pilgrim, burthened with thy sin,
    Come the way to Zion's gate,
There till mercy lets thee in,
    Knock, and weep, and watch, and wait;
    Knock!—He knows the sinner's cry;
    Weep!—He loves the mourner's tear;
Watch!—for saving grace is nigh;
    Wait!—till heavenly light appear.

2 Hark! it is the Bridegroom's voice;
    Welcome, pilgrim, to thy rest;
Now within the gate rejoice,
    Safe, and sealed, and bought, and blest.
Safe—from all the lures of vice,
    Sealed—by signs the chosen know,
Bought—by love, and life the price,
    Blest—the mighty debt to owe.—*Crabbe.*

1 Holy Father, hear my cry;
    Holy Savior, bend Thine ear;
Holy Spirit, come Thou nigh:
    Father, Savior, Spirit, hear.
Father, save me from my sin,
    Savior, I Thy mercy crave;
Gracious Spirit, make me clean:
    Father, Son, and Spirit, save.

2 Father, let me taste Thy love;
    Savior, fill my soul with peace;
Spirit, come my heart to move:
    Father, Son, and Spirit, bless!
Father, Son, and Spirit—thou
    One Jehovah, shed abroad
All Thy grace within me now;
    Be my Father and my God.

D. W. MILLER.

1. Lord, I bring to Thee my chain, Heav-ier bonds on Thee are flung;
2. Lord, my guard on per - ils brink, Be my guide thro' weal or woe;

Bare to me Thy bo-som's pain, Bit - t'rer pangs from Thee were wrung.
Teach me of Thy cup to drink, Make me in Thy path to go.

I re - call that aw - ful hour, When the Shepherd of the flock,
What is earth - ly change or loss, With Thy prom - ise still mine own?

Prince of Peace, the Lord of Power, Was the sol - dier's mock.
E - ven I may bear Thy cross, I may share Thy throne.

GOD KNOWS IT ALL.

D. W. MILLER.

1. In the dim re-cess of thy spir-it's cham-ber, Is there some
2. And art thou tossed on bil-lows of temp-ta - tion, And wouldst do
3. Art thou oppress'd,and poor, and heav-y - heart-ed, The heavens a -

si - lent grief thou may'st not tell? Let not thy heart for -
good, but e - vil oft pre - vails? Oh, think a - mid the
bove thee in thick clouds ar - rayed? And well nigh crushed,no

sake thee, but re - mem-ber His pity - ing eye, who
waves of trib - u - la - tion, When earth - ly hopes, and
earth - ly thought im - part-ed, No friend - ly voice to

sees and knows it well.
earth - ly ref - uge fails, God knows it all! God knows it all.
say "Be not a - fraid?"

4 Dost thou look back upon a life of sinning,
Forward, and tremble for thy future lot?
There's One who sees the end from the beginning,
Thy tear of penitence is unforgot.
God knows it all!

5 Then go to God, pour out your heart before him,
There is no grief your Father can not feel;
And let your grateful songs of praise adore him,
To save, forgive, and every wound to heal.
God knows it all!

D. W. MILLER.

1. Though earth is my dwell - ing, it is not my home,
2. Oh, ma - ny a beau - ty has this world of ours,

I look for a hap - pi-er king-dom to come, Where the Savior is
With its sunlight, its harvests, its sheaves, and its flowers; But thorns are at-

sent - ed with an-gels in light, For in heaven is no dan - ger,
tached to the love-li - est rose, And in heav-en a - lone will

CHORUS.

no sor-row, nor night. Home, sweet home, home, sweet home, sweet home.
be per - fect re - pose.

3 There is nought on this earth that can free us from care,
For thistles and briars spring up every-where;
Then why should we mourn for the frail things of earth,
When we hope for a home that has far greater worth?

1. All hail the pow'r of Je-sus' name, Let an-gels pros-trate fall;

Bring forth the roy - al di - a - dem, And crown Him Lord of all, Bring

forth the roy - al di - a - dem, And crown Him Lord of all.

2 Ye chosen seed of Israel's race,
Ye ransomed from the fall,
Hail Him, who saves you by His grace,
And crown Him Lord of all.

3 Sinners, whose love can ne'er forget
The wormwood and the gall,
Go, spread your trophies at His feet,
And crown Him Lord of all.

4 Let every kindred, every tribe,
On this terrestrial ball,
To Him all majesty ascribe,
And crown Him Lord of all.

5 Oh, that with yonder sacred throng
We at His feet may fall;
We'll join the everlasting song,
And crown Him Lord of all.

1 Come, let us join our cheerful songs,
With angels round the throne;
Ten thousand thousand are their
But all their joys are one. [tongues,

2 "Worthy the Lamb that died," they
"To be exalted thus." [cry,
"Worthy the Lamb," our lips reply,
"For He was slain for us."

3 Let all that dwell above the sky,
And air, and earth, and seas,
Conspire to lift Thy glories high,
And speak Thine endless praise.

4 The whole creation join in one,
To bless the Sacred name
Of Him who sits upon the throne,
And to adore the Lamb.

Arranged.

When I sur-vey the won-drous cross On
which the Prince of glo-ry died, My rich-est gain I
count but loss, And pour con-tempt on all my pride.

1 When I survey the wondrous cross
On which the Prince of glory died,
My richest gain I count but loss,
And pour contempt on all my pride.

2 Forbid it, Lord, that I should boast,
Save in the death of Christ, my God;
All the vain things that charm me most,
I sacrifice them to His blood. [most,

3 See, from His head, His hands, His feet,
Sorrow and love flow mingled down!
Did e'er such love and sorrow meet,
Or thorns compose so rich a crown?

4 Were the whole realm of nature mine,
That were a present far too small;
Love so amazing, so divine,
Demands my soul, my life, my all.

THE PENITENT RESTORED.

1 O Thou that hear'st when sinners cry,
Though all my crimes before Thee lie,
Behold them not with angry look,
But blot their memory from Thy book.

2 My soul lies humbled in the dust,
And owns Thy dreadful sentence just:
Look down, O Lord, with pitying eye,
And save the soul condemned to die.

3 Tho' I have grieved Thy Spirit, Lord,
His health and comfort still afford,
And let a wretch come near Thy throne,
To plead the merits of Thy Son.

4 I can not live without Thy light,
Cast out and banished from Thy sight;
Thy holy joys, my God, restore,
And guard me that I fall no more.

1 My country, tis of thee,
  Sweet land of liberty,
    Of thee I sing:
  Land where my fathers died,
  Land of the pilgrim's pride,
    From every mountain side
    Let freedom ring.

2 My native country, thee,
  Land of the noble free,
    Thy name I love:
  I love thy rocks and rills,
  Thy woods and templed hills;
  My heart with rapture thrills
    Like that above.

3 Let music swell the breeze,
  And ring from all the trees
    Sweet freedom's song:
  Let mortal tongues awake,
  Let all that breathe partake,
  Let rocks their silence break,
    The sound prolong.

4 Our father's God to thee,
  Author of liberty,
    To thee we sing:
  Long may our land be bright
  With freedom's holy light,
  Protect us by thy might,
    Great God, our King.
      S. F. SMITH, 1833.

1 God bless our native land,
  Firm may she ever stand
    Through storm and night;
  When the wild tempests rave,
  Ruler of wind and wave,
  Do Thou our country save
    By Thy great might.

2 For her our prayer shall rise
  To God, above the skies,
    On Him we wait:
  Thou who art ever nigh,
  Guarding with watchful eye,
  To Thee aloud we cry,
    God, save the state.
      JNO. S. DWIGHT, 1844.

DR. L. MASON.

Oh, could I speak the matchless worth; Oh, could I sound the glories
I'd sing the precious blood He spilt My ransom from the dreadful

forth, Which in my Sav-iour shine, I'd soar and touch the
guilt Of sin and wrath di-vine: I'd sing His glo-rious

heav'n-ly strings, And vie with Ga-briel, while he sings, In
right-eous-ness, In which all-per-fect, heav'n-ly dress My

notes al-most di-vine, In notes al-most di-vine.
soul shall ev-er shine, My soul shall ev-er shine.

3 I'd sing the characters He bears,
And all the forms of love He wears,
　Exalted on His throne;
In loftiest songs of sweetest praise,
I would to everlasting days
　Make all His glories known.

4 Soon the delightful day will come
When my dear Lord will call me home,
　And I shall see His face;
Then, with my Saviour, Brother, Friend,
A blest eternity I'll spend,
　Triumphant in His grace.

IN HIS KEEPING.

CALISTA L. GRANT.   D. W. MILLER.

1. I lay me down at night In peaceful sleep, And care not if the glorious

morning light Should never greet again this mortal sight-My soul he'll keep! The

ev - er - last-ing arms En-cir - cle me: I can not fall beneath them

in life's storms, I'm safe from all that leads astray or harms, So strong is he!

2 On him my cares I lay
   Whate'er betides;
 Whether I tread a long and shadowed way,
 Or swift am borne by angels bright away,
   'Tis he who guides.
 If I my waking find
   Within the vail,
 All doubt and darkness will be left behind,
 I'll trust the hand that hath been always kind—
   God can not fail.

JERUSALEM, THE BEAUTIFUL.

Rev. M. L. HOFFORD.　　　　　　　　　　D. W. MILLER.

1. Je - ru - sa - lem, the beau-ti-ful! Its glo - ries are un-told, Its
2. Je - ru - sa - lem, the beau-ti-ful! Its gates are pearl-y white, To

walls are built of pre-cious stones, Its pavements made of gold; Its
voice of prayer and song of praise, Are o - pen day and night; And

man-sions for the ran-somed ones In match-less splendor shine. Je -
shin-ing ones a - round the throne In sweet-er rapt-ure sing, Je -

ru - sa - lem, the beau - ti - ful! Je - ru - sa - lem di - vine.
ru - sa - lem, the beau - ti - ful! When saints their trib-ute bring.

3 Jerusalem, the beautiful!
　From thy celestial throng
Familiar voices reach mine ear,
　Enraptured in thy song;
And, oh, it were transporting
　To soar aloft and see
Jerusalem, the beautiful!
　And join thy jubilee.

4 Jerusalem, the beautiful!
　My everlasting rest!
The glorious home of mine abode,
　The city of the blest;
Thy temple is the living one,
　Thy light is all divine.
Jerusalem, the beautiful!
　I love to call thee mine.

THE GLORY TO BE REVEALED.

E. S. W.

D. W. MILLER.

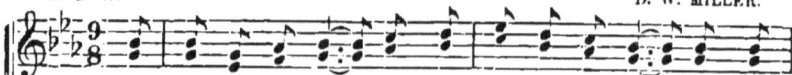

1. Ah! lit - tle I'll reck when the jour-ney is o'er, Of the
2. Then why should I trem-ble when tossed on the wave? For the

burdens and griefs I so dreaded and bore; They'll all be forgot as I
Lord full in sight, and my
fierc-est of storms can not give me a grave While Jesus is pres - ent to
rag - ing the o - cean, the

en - ter the door. With my
self with - out stain, Oh, how bliss-ful the notes, how tri-
com - fort and save. And though
skies are se - rene; Tho' the clouds dark - ly gath - er, the

umph-ant the strain, As my tongue sounds His praises again and a-gain.
sun shines be-tween, And bright o'er the billows "The Cit-y" is seen.

3 My hope is in God! then, my heart, be at rest;
The waves swell in wrath, but each glittering crest
Is bright with the glory encircling His breast.
He reigns! and He loves me! no longer I roam,
Remembering the music and light 'round the throne,
So soon to be mine when the journey is done.

LOOK NO MORE WITHIN.

I. E. RANKIN, D. D.   D. W. MILLER.

1. Look no more with - in, There is on - ly sin!
2. Look no more with - in, There is on - ly sin!
3. Look no more with - in, There is on - ly sin!

Lost, the Fa - ther could not have you, So His on - ly
Cast the sad, sad past be - hind you, Let the tempt - er
Help from self you can not bor - row, Nor a - tone for

Son He gave you; Look to Je - sus, He will save you;
no more blind you, Nor with - in his pris - ons grind you;
sin and sor - row; Nor make read - y for the mor - row;

Look to Him, the work is done: You are saved in Christ the Son.
Call earth's rich - est gain but loss; Fix your eyes up - on the cross.
He will bear your sins a - way, He's God's new and liv - ing way.

4 Look no more within,
　　There is only sin!
　　All your help from self disowning,
　　Leave your sighing and your groaning;
　　Look to Christ, the Lamb atoning,
　　He will bear your sins away,
　　He's God's new and living way.

O LIGHT OF LIGHT.

Words arranged.

D. W. MILLER.

1. O Light of light, shine in! Cast out this night of sin, Create true day with - in; O Light of light, shine in! O Joy of joys, come in! End Thou this grief of sin, Create calm peace with - in; O Joy of joys, come in!

2 O Life of life, pour in!
Expel this death of sin,
  Awake true life within;
O Life of life, pour in!
O Love of love, flow in!
  This hateful root of sin
  Pluck up, destroy within;
O Love of love, flow in!

HORATIUS BONAR.

D. W. MILLER.

1. I come, I rest beneath The shadow of His wing, That I may know How good it is Here to a - bide; How safe its shel-ter-ing; I lean against the cross When fainting by the way; It bears my weight, It holds me up, It cheers my soul, It turns my night to day.

2 I Clasp the outstretched hand
Of my delivering Lord;
Unto His arm
I lean myself—
His arm divine—
It doth me help afford.
I hear the gracious words
He speaketh to my soul;
They whisper rest,
They banish fear.
They say "Be strong;"
They make my spirit whole.

TAKE CHRIST ON BOARD.

Words arranged.

D. W. MILLER.

1. Take Christ on board thy lit - tle ship, Trust thou in Him a - lone; Push

from the shore, fear not the waves That break with sullen moan. Altho' thy vessel

trembles sore With angry tossing more and more, Still, tho' the waters raging

Rit.

be, And do increase, Yet be at peace, For Christ is with thee on the sea.

2 If midst the howling of the storm
  Thou canst not hold the helm.
  Have courage, for He will not let
  The waves thee overwhelm.
Yet though the waves surge very high,
The thunder roll, the lightning fly,
Thy ship in safety on will sail;
  Upheaving crest
  Will be at rest
When Christ is with thee in the gale.

3 Awake, awake! be watching, aye,
  Hope, trust in Him and pray,
  And Christ, the Lord, in His good time
  The tempest will allay.
The storm is silent at his voice,
Therefore, oh, timid child, rejoice:
The wildest waves at length will cease
  At His command;
  And in His hand
He holds the rainbow of our peace!

Words arranged.
Slowly and tenderly.

D. W. MILLER.

1. There's only One on whose dear arm We safely lay our tho'ts to rest; There's only One who knows the depth Of sorrow in each stricken breast. There's only One who whose pit-y falls Like dew upon the wounded heart; There's on-ly One who never stirs, Though en-e-my and friend de-part.

2 There's only One when none are by
    To wipe away the falling tear;
  There's only One to heal the wound,
    And stay the weak one's timid fear.
  There's only One who understands
    And enters into all we feel;
  There's only One who views each spring
    And each perplexing wheel in wheel.

3 There's only One who can support,
    And who sufficient grace can give
  To bear up under every grief,
    And spotless in this world to live.
  There's only One who will abide
    When loved ones in the grave are cold;
  There's only One who'll go with me
    When this long, painful journey 's done.

THE TOUCH OF JESUS.

Words arranged.

D. W. MILLER.

1. O Je - sus, for a touch di-vine To rest up-on this frame of mine! As

now I lie, an emp-ty cup, With vig-'rous life, oh, fill me up; Touch

Thou mine eyes, that I may see What Thou wouldst have me do and be; Touch

Thou my lips, my feet, my hands, That they may fol-low Thy commands.

2 Touch Thou my heart, and flaming fire
Shall burst and blaze, and life inspire,
And circle 'round my home below,
And every moment brighter glow;
A flame to brighten like the sun,
And warm and cheer me while I run;
To do Thy will through all the day,
In even, or in roughest way.

Words arranged.

D. W. MILLER.

1. Anywhere with Jesus, says the Christian heart, Let Him take me where He will,

so we do not part; Always sitting at his feet, there's no cause for fears,

An-y-where with Je-sus in this vale of tears. An-ywhere with Jesus!

CHORUS.

an-y-where with Je-sus! A-ny-where! an-y-where! any-where with Jesus!

2 Anywhere with Jesus, though He leadeth me
Where the path be rough and long, where the dangers be;
Though He take away from me all I love below,
Anywhere with Jesus will I gladly go.—CHORUS.

3 Anywhere with Jesus, for it can not be
Dreary, dark, or desolate, where He is with me;
He will love me alway, every need supply;
Anywhere with Jesus, should I live or die.—CHORUS.

I LOVE JESUS.

Words arranged.

D. W. MILLER.

1. I love, I love Jesus, I love, I love Jesus, My soul's supreme delight;
2. I love, I love Jesus, I love, I love Jesus, Because He first loved me;

At ear - ly morn-ing hour, and late at night, In prayers
And heaven and earth will pass a - way, and be As things

and tears and vows, to Thee I plight My troth, my love.
that were, ere I shall ev - er see Change in His love.

I love, I love Jesus, I love, I love Jesus, My soul's supreme delight.
I love, I love Jesus, I love, I love Jesus, Because He first loved me.

3 I love, I love Jesus,
I love, I love Jesus,
He is my all in all;
With patience, faith, and hope I wait the call,
When I into the folding arms may fall,
   Of Christ, my love.
I love, I love Jesus,
I love, I love Jesus,
He is my all in all.

Words arranged.   D. W. MILLER.

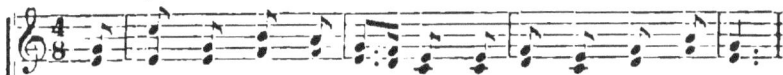

1. To search for truth and wis - dom, To live for Christ a - lone;
2. To shun the world's al - lurements, To bear my cross there-in;
3. To keep my troth un - shak - en, Tho' oth - ers may de-ceive;

To run my race un - bur - ened, The goal my Sav - ior's throne;
To turn from all temp - ta - tion, To con - quer ev - 'ry sin;
To give with will - ing pleas-ure, Or still with joy re - ceive;

To view by faith the prom-ise, While earth - ly hopes de - cay;
To lin - ger, calm and pa - tient. Where du - ty bids me stay;
To bring the mourn- er com - fort, To wipe sad tears a - way;

To serve the Lord with glad-ness—This is my work to - day.
To go where God may lead me—This is my work to - day.
To help the tim - id doubt - er—This is my work to - day.

4 To bear another's weakness,
    To soothe another's pain ;
  To cheer the heart repentant,
    And to forgive again;
  To commune with the thoughtful,
    To guide the young and gay ;
  To profit all in season—
    This is my work to-day.

5 I think not of to-morrow.
    Its trial or its task ;
  But still with childlike spirit
    For present mercies ask ;
  With each returning morning
    I cast old things away ;
  Life's journey lies before me—
    My prayer is for to-day.

COME UNTO ME.

ELEANOR KIRK.   D. W. MILLER.

1. A sweet-er song than e'er was sung By po-et, priest, or sa-ges, A
2. Oh! wise provision, sweet command, Vouchsafed the weak and weary; A
3. "Come unto me," the way's not long, His hands are stretched to meet thee; Now

song which, thro' all heav'n has rung. And down thro' all the a - ges; A
friend to find on eith-er hand A light for pros - pect dreary; A
still thy sobbing, list the song Which ev'rywhere shall greet thee. Here

precious strain of sweet accord. A note of cheer from Christ our Lord: List!
Friend who knows our bit-ter need, Of each endeav - or tak-ing heed: Who
at His feet your bur-den lay, Why 'neath it bend another day, Since

as it vibrates full and free, Oh, grieving heart "come unto me." Come
calls to ev -'ry soul opprest, "Come unto me, I ll give you rest" Come
One so lov - ing calls to thee, "Oh, heav-y la-den, come to me, "Come

Rit.

un - to me, come un - to me, Oh, grieving heart, come unto me.
un - to me, come un - to me, Oh, grieving heart, come unto me.
un - to me, come un - to me, Oh, grieving heart, come unto me.

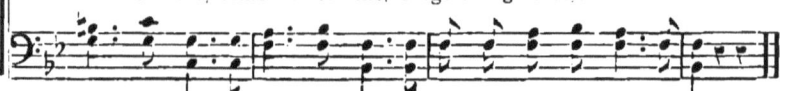

EVA M. TAPPAN.   D. W. MILLER.

1. Oh, what shall I give to my Sav-iour For
what He hath giv'n for me? I'll give Him the
gift of an earn-est life, Of a heart that is
lov-ing and free from strife; As He hath giv'n for me.

2. And what shall I do for my Sav-iour For
what He hath done for me? I'll pray for the
sick and the e-vil doer; And I'll make for my
friends those a-mong the poor, As He hath done for me.

3 And what shall I bear for the Saviour,
  For what He hath borne for me?
Remembering I'm his constant care;
And whatever He sends me I will bear,
  As He hath borne for me.

4 And what shall I be for the Saviour,
  For what He hath been for me?
Long-suffering, kind, unselfish, pure;
To believe, and to bear, to hope, endure,
  As he hath been for me.

STAR OF BETHLEHEM.

D. W. MILLER.

1. As with glad-ness men of old Did the guid-ing star be-hold,
2. As with joy-ful steps they sped To that ho-ly man-ger bed,

As with joy they hailed its light Lead-ing on-ward, beaming bright,
There to bend the knee be-fore Him, whom heav'n and earth a-dore,

So, most gracious God, may we Ev-er-more be led by Thee,
So may we with will-ing feet Ev-er seek Thy mer-cy-seat,

So, most gra-cious God, may we Ev-er-more be led by Thee.
So may we with will-ing feet Ev-er seek Thy mer-cy-seat.

3 As they offered gifts most rare,
At that manger. rude and bare,
So may we with holy joy,
Pure and free from sin's alloy,
{:Our celestial treasures bring.
Christ, to Thee, our heavenly King.:}

4 Holy Jesus, every day
Keep us in the narrow way;
And when earthly things are past,
Bring our ransomed souls at last
{: Where they need no star to guide,
Where no clouds Thy glory hide.:}

Words arranged.
Alto Solo. Slowly.

D. W. MILLER.

1. Now the sol-emn shadows dark-en, And the day-light slowly dies;

Ho - ly Saviour, Thou wilt hearken When Thy children's pray'rs a-rise.

Bless-ed Je - sus, bless-ed Je - sus, Look on us with lov - ing eyes,

Bless-ed Je - sus, bless-ed Je - sus, Look on us with lov - ing eyes.

2 When our earthly day is closing,
  And the night grows still and deep,
Let us in thine arms reposing,
  Feel thy power to save and keep.
    ‖: Blessed Jesus, Blessed Jesus,
  Give Thine own beloved sleep. :‖

THE SHADOW OF THE ROCK.

Words arranged.

D. W. MILLER.

1. In the shad-ow of the Rock Let me rest, let me rest; When I
2. On the parched and desert way Where I tread, where I tread, With the
3. I in peace will rest me there Till I see, till I see That the

feel the tem-pest's shock Thrill my breast, thrill my breast, All in
scorching noon-tide ray O'er my head, o'er my head, Let my
skies a - gain are fair O - ver me, o - ver me; And with

vain the storm shall sweep, I'll my tranquil station keep; I'll abide while I hide
weary steps be stayed, While I find the welcome shade; I'll abide while I hide
joyous heart and strong I will raise to Thee a song—I'll abide while I hide

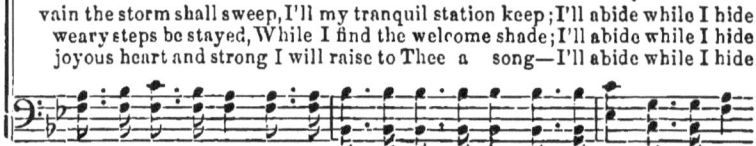

CHORUS.

by Thy side, by Thy side.
by Thy side, by Thy side. In the shad-ow of the Rock, In the
by Thy side, by Thy side.

shad-ow of the Rock, I'll a-bide while I hide by Thy side, by Thy side.

BUILT ON THE SUREST FOUNDATION. 41

Words arranged.

D. W. MILLER.

1. Built on the surest founda-tion, "In Christ," where's no condemnation,
2. Liv-ing my life of pro - ba- tion, One of Christ's own 'holy na-tion,"
3. Knowing from whence I was taken, Never can I be for-sak - en;
4. Fighting with sins most besetting, Hating the world, and for - get-ting;

Safe in His per - fect sal - va - tion, By His grace I will stand.
Kept in the hour of temp-ta - tion, By His grace I will stand.
My heart shall al-ways a - wak - en, By His grace I will stand.
My love on Christ I am set - ting, By His grace I will stand.

CHORUS.

By His grace I will stand Safe in His per-fect sal -va - tion;

Built on the sur-est foun-da - tion, By His grace I will stand.

5 Why, then, should I be distressed,
   My soul with sorrow oppressed?
   I trust in His name, and am blessed,
      By His grace I will stand.

6 Resting on Christ, He will never
   His hands clasped around me dissever;
   Once His, it must be forever,
      By His grace I will stand.

IN THE CLEFT.

Words arranged.

D. W. MILLER.

1. When my heart is like to break, When the surg-ing bil-lows shake,
2. When I see my sins so great, When no com-fort I can get,
3. When no ref - uge I can find, And despair o'erwhelms the mind,

Lead me to the Rock most high, The Rock that higher is than I.
Lead me to the Rock most high, The Rock that higher is than I.
Lead me to the Rock most high, The Rock that higher is than I.

CHORUS.

In the cleft, in the cleft, In the cleft of that dear Rock,

In the cleft of that dear Rock, Safe from ev -'ry tempest's shock.

4 When I'm thirsting for the stream
Of eternal life in him,
Lead me to the Rock most high,
The Rock that higher is than I.

5 In that righteousness so pure,
In that covenant so sure,
In the cleft of that dear Rock,
I'm safe from every tempest's shock.

D. W. MILLER.   D. W. MILLER.

1. "Ask, and ye shall re-ceive," The Sav-iour is say-ing to you,
2. Ask, and on-ly be-lieve, For all things are promised to you,
3. "Seek, ye sure-ly shall find;" And "Knock, it shall o-pen to you;"

"What-so-ev-er ye shall ask In my name, will I do."
"No good thing will he with-hold" From those whose love is true.
Gra-cious words; what more can I Ask Him for me to do.

Refrain.

With Thy sweet promise in my heart I can not go a-miss;

Thou, and on-ly Thou canst give To me com-plet-est bliss.

4 Jesus, show me the way,
Thy will both to know and to do;
More to love thy sweet commands,
And to obey them too.—REF.

5 Yield I myself to Thee,
My every desire thou dost know;
Thy good gifts are freely giv'n
To all on earth below.—REF.

1. I'll come to Thee, O Jesus Christ. I'll Thy disciple be; Not
2. I'll strive to do Thy bless-ed will, Renounce my will-ful ways, An
3. I'll fol-low Thee, to watch Thy way From manger on to grave; Fo

tears, not deeds, but self I'll bring. Be-cause Thou call-est me. I'll
live a life, though stained by sin. More worthy of Thy grace. I'll
step by step 'tis thus I learn Thy sovereign pow'r to save. I

come a-lone to hear Thy word. And at Thy feet I'll rest; For
hope thro' all my mor-tal days Thee by my side to find; To
know that Thou Thy Spir-it's help From me wilt ne'er with-hold; So

while I hear no voice be-side. I'm cheered, I'm helped, I'm blest.
feast my eyes, to free my heart. To beau-ti-fy my mind.
all the vic-t'ries of my life By tongue can ne'er be told.

4 Then brighter far than summer's sun,
  More glad than marriage joy,
In serving, praising, crowning Thee,
  Eternal life employ.
I'll sing Thee here, my Spirit's Prince,
  And follow in Thy train,
Until Thy will my place shall change,
  And death shall be my gain.

HOW SWEET TO TRUST IN JESUS.

45

Words arranged.

D. W. MILLER.

1. How sweet to trust in Je - sus, To know no trust be - side; To
2. How sweet to fol - low Je - sus, To seek no oth - er road; O -
3. Ah! then to learn of Je - sus, This is a task most sweet! To

find in Him a ref - uge, Our wea - ry souls to hide; To
be - dient - ly and trust - ing, To walk the path He trod; 'Tis
choose the "bet - ter por - tion," Like Ma - ry at His feet. To

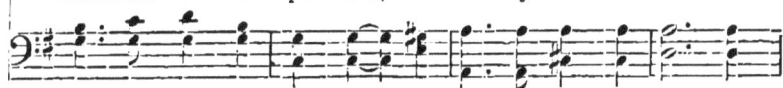

lean on love e - ter - nal, And in that love a - bide; How
hal - lowed by His foot - prints, And nigh - est un - to God; How
seek a con - se - cra - tion, For His blest use made meet; How

sweet to trust in Je - sus, To trust in none be - side.
sweet to fol - low Je - sus, To fol - low none be - side.
sweet to learn of Je - sus, To learn of none be - side.

4 'Tis sweet to work for Jesus,
  To spread abroad His fame;
To be His living witnesses,
  Bearing His cross and shame,
That to the lost and dying
  His love we may proclaim;
How sweet to work for Jesus,
  To work for none beside.

HE CARES FOR ME.

Words arranged.   D. W. MILLER.

1. He cares for me, why do I fret At ev-'ry lit-tle ill, And
2. Peace in my heart, what shall I fear While I so-journ be-low? He

vex my-self so needless-ly? O, rest-less heart, be still. Rest-
will de-fend me in the fight From ev-'ry com-ing foe. Let

ing on Him, then let me stay Up-on His hope-ful word; Faith-
friends be cold, or foes be wroth, And bit-ter mal-ice cast, My

ful are all the prom-is-es Of our dear lov-ing Lord.
Sav-iour, 'midst a hat-ing world Loved me e'en to the last.

3 He cares for me, oh, wondrous grace!
  Lord, fill my barren heart
With love divine for all thy love;
  Bid all my sin depart.
The lilies and the snow-drops grow
  In lowly beauty rare,
But He will clothe me in His robe
  Of righteousness, so fair.

4 I come to Thee! Jesus, I cast
  My cares and fears on Thee;
Rid me of self and earthliness,
  From sin, oh, set me free.
Then to my Father's house me bring,
  That holy dwelling-place,
To love, to serve, to praise Thee there,
  And see Thy loving face.

NOT FAR FROM THE KINGDOM.

To be read.

A ship came sailing and sailing
Over a murmuring sea,
And just in sight of the haven
Down in the waves went she!

And the spars and the broken timbers
Were cast on a storm-beat strand;
And a cry went up in the darkness,
Not far, not far from the land.

Words arranged.

D. W. MILLER.

1. Not far, not far from the Kingdom, Yet in the shadow of sin;
2. Catching the strain of the mu-sic Float-ing so sweetly a-long,

How ma-ny are com-ing and go-ing, How few are en-ter-ing in?
E'en knowing the song they are sing-ing, Yet join-ing not in the song.

Not far from the gold-en gate-way, There voices whisper and wait;
And seek-ing the warmth and beau-ty, The in-fi-nite love and light,

Fear-ing to en-ter in bold-ly, So lin-ger-ing still at the gate.
Yet wea-ry, lonely, and wait-ing, Still out in the des-o-late night.

3 Out in the dark and the danger,
   Out in the night and the cold;
And though He is longing to lead them
   So tenderly to the fold.
Not far, not far from the Kingdom,
   'Tis only now a short space;
Oh, let it not be forever,
   Still out of the sweet resting-place.

48 HARK! WHAT MEAN THOSE HOLY VOICES.

D. W. MILLER.

1. Hark! what mean those holy voic - es Sweetly sound-ing thro' the skies?
2. Peace on earth, good-will from heaven, Reaching far as man is found!

Lo! th' an-gel - ic host re-joic - es, Loudest hal - le - lu-jahs rise.
Souls redeemed, and sins for - giv - en, Loud our golden harps shall sound

List - en to the wondrous story Which they chant in hymns of
Christ is born, the great Anointed! Heav'n and earth His praises

joy: Glo - ry in the highest, glo - ry! Glo - ry be to God most high
sing; Glad receive whom God appointed For your Prophet, Priest, and King

3 Hasten, mortals to adore Him,
    Learn His name and taste His joy,
Till in heaven you sing before Him
    Glory be to God most high!
Let us learn the wondrous story
    Of our great Redeemer's birth;
Spread the brightness of His glory
    Till it cover all the earth.—Jno. Cawood, 1819.

Words arranged.

D. W. MILLER.

1. My sleepless eyes were dim with tears, My heart was sad with nameless fears; Then One I know not
2. But He, the loving Friend and true, Soon gave me sterner work to do; Led me in-to the
3. He came, the strong De-liverer, And made me more than conqueror; His love, a pow'r with-

came to me, And saved my soul from mis - er - y. The radiance of that Light di-vine In
wil - der-ness To trace the way of ho - li - ness. I met the tempter, felt his pow'r, And
in, my heart Scatheless be-came to Sa - tan's art. And now I walk the earth a king, Crowned

to my night of gloom did shine; I saw the One who died for me; To turn and look so
yield-ed in an e - vil hour; crushed, bleeding, guilty, helpless lay, Far from the straight and
with the thorns of suf-fer - ing; Wearing the robe that Je-sus wore, Bear - ing the heav-y

lov - ing - ly, Ec - stat - ic joy my be - ing thrilled! Glo - ry the earth and
nar - row way; Out of the depths of my de - spair I cried to God to
cross He bore; Wait - ing to join the count-less throng That sing heav'n's ju - bi -

sun may bring Some pen-i-ten - tial of - fer - ing; In Thy de
throne may rise Sweet incense from some sac - ri - fice; Up - lift-ed

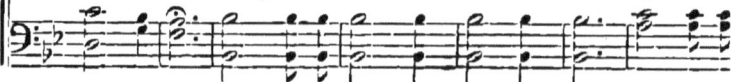

name some kind - ness done, To Thy dear love some wand'rer wo
eyes, undimmed by tears; Up - lift - ed faith, unstained by fear

Some tri-al meek - ly borne for Thee, Dear Lord, for Thee, dear Lord, for The
Hail-ing each joy as light from Thee, Dear Lord, for Thee, dear Lord, for The

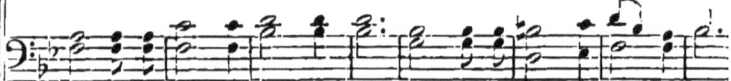

3 Something, my God, for Thee,
   Something for Thee;
For the great love that Thou hast given,
For the dear hope of Thee and heaven,
My soul its first allegiance brings,
While full of faith and love it sings,
And upward plumes its heavenward wings
   Dear Lord, to Thee, dear Lord, to Thee.

STAR OF THE EAST.

D. W. MILLER.

BOYS. Not too fast.

{ Star of the East, the ho - ri - zon a - dorning, Guide where our infant Redeemer is laid;
{ Brightest and best of the sons of the morning, Dawn on our darkness and lend us Thine aid.

GIRLS.

Cold on His cra-dle the dewdrops are shining, Low lies His head with the beasts of the stall;

BOYS.

Star of the East, the horizon adorning, Guide where our infant Redeemer is laid.

CHORUS. Slow and soft.

An - gels a - dore Him, in slum - ber re-clin-ing,

Mak - er and Mon - arch, and Sav - iour of all.

Sprightly.

Say, shall we yield Him, in costly devo-tion, O-dors of E - dom, off'rings divi

Gems of the mountain, and pearls of the ocean, Myrrh from the forest or gold fro
the min

CHORUS. Slow and soft.

Cold   on   His cra - dle   the   dew - drops are shin-ing,

Low   lies His   head   with the   beasts   of   the stall;

DUET.

Vain-ly we   of - fer each am-ple ob - la-tion, Vainly with gold would Hi se - cure; Rich - er by far is the heart's ad - o - ra - tion,

CHORUS. Marching time.

to God are the pray'rs of the poor. Brightest and best of the

the morn-ing, Dawn on our dark - ness and lend us Thine aid.

the East, tho ho - ri - zon a - dorning, Guide where our infant Re-

is laid, Guide where our in - fant Re-deem - er is laid.

love, Till the crown the cross repla - ces In Gods happy land a
thing, So heav-y to lift and to car-ry, It could on - ly wear-ines

bove. 'Tis the ho - ly bond of union Between my Saviour and me 'Tis
bring; But when I stooped to the burden, And took it within my arms; I

on - ly by bearing it dai - ly His heaven - ly face I see.
found it grew ea - sy to car - ry I saw it had hid - den charms.

3 And as I carried it oftener,
Daily uplifting it high,
Before I knew, it had lifted
Me 'tween the earth and the sky.
Under me now is the vast world,
I stand upon Zion s crest;
I am linked to the cross forever,
Beside it I sweetly rest.

THE SINNER'S PLEA.

Words arranged.   D. W. MILLER.

1. My sin is great, my strength is weak, My path be-set with
2. The world is dark with-out Thee, Lord, I turn me from its

snares; But Thou, O Christ, hast died for me, And Thou wilt hear my pray'rs.
strife, To find Thy love a sweet re-lief; Thou art the light of life.

Refrain.

To Thee, my Sav-iour, cru-ci-fied, The sin-ner's on-ly

plea; Re-ly-ing on Thy promised grace, I come, I come to Thee.

3 Temptations lure and foes assail
  My frail, inconstant heart:
But precious are Thy promises,
  And Thou new strength impart.

4 Unfold Thy precepts to my mind,
  And cleanse my blinded eyes;
Grant me to work for Thee on earth,
  Then praise Thee in the skies.

BEHOLD! I KNOCK.

Words arranged.   D. W. MILLER.

1. Be-hold, I knock! be-hold, I knock! O soul, art thou at
2. Be-hold, I knock! be-hold, I knock! Say not, "'tis zeph-yr
3. Be-hold, I knock! be-hold, I knock! As yet I am the

home? for thy be-lov-ed's here; Hast thou made ready flow'rs ereHe should
mild which rus-tles the dead leaf." It is the Sav-iour, 'tis thy God, my
guest wait-ing without for thee; The time shall come, when homeless and dis-

come? Is thy lamp burning clear? Know'st thou how such a Friend received should
child, Let not thine ear be deaf. If I come now in breez-es soft and
tressed, Thou, soul shall knock for me! To those who heard my voice ere 'twas too

be? Art thou in brid-al garments dress'd for me? Deck'd with thy jewels
warm, I may re-turn a-gain up-on the storm; 'Tis no light fan-cy—
late, I o-pen in that hour my peaceful gate; To those who scorned, a

as for guests most dear? Be-hold, I knock! be-hold, I knock!
firm be thy be-lief. Be-hold, I knock! be-hold, I knock!
closed door will it be, Be-hold, I knock! be-hold, I knock!

SABBATH REST.

Words arranged.

D. W. MILLER.

1. Sab - bath of the saints of old, Day of mys-t'ries
2. Rest - ing from His work, the Lord Spake to - day the
3. Rest - ing from His work to - day, In the tomb the

man - i - fold, By the great cre - a - tor blest,
hal - lowed word, And the won - drous la - bors done;
Sav - iour lay; Still He slept: from head to feet,

Type of His e - ter - nal rest, I with thoughts of
Thou, the ev - er - last - ing Son, Gave to heav'n and
Shroud-ed in the wind - ing sheet, Ly - ing in the

Thee would seek T' sanc - ti - fy the clos - ing week.
earth a sign Of a won - der more di - vine.
rock a lone, Hid - den by the seal - ed stone.

4 Late at even there was seen
Watching long, the Magdalene;
Early, ere the break of day,
Sorrowful she took her way
To the holy garden glade
Where her buried Lord was laid.

5 So with Thee till life shall end
I would solem vigil spend
Let me hew Thee, Lord, a shrine
In this rocky heart of mine;
Where in pure embalmed cell
None but Thee may ever dwell.

I NEED THEE.

D. W. MILLER.   D. W. MILLER.

1. Je - sus, ev - 'ry day and hour Do I need Thy love and
2. Yes! I need Thy Spir - its cheer, Need Thy sym - pa - thiz - ing

power, Need Thy wis-dom me to guide. Need Thy goodness to pro-
tear, Need Thee in the try - ing hour Of the tempter's e - vil

vide. Need Thee as the on - ly light In the dark - ness of the
power, Need Thee in my joy and grief, Need Thy prom-ise for re-

night, Need Thy presence in my heart, O do Thou more faith im-part.
lief; Need Thy blood to cleanse my soul, Need Thy grace to make me whole

3 Jesus, every day and hour
Do I need Thy love and power,
Need Thee till my feet shall be
Planted by the crystal sea,
Need Thee, ever blessed Lamb,
Till I bear the victor's palm;
Need thee, till my soul shall be
Wholly swallowed up in Thee.

D. W. MILLER.

1. Hearts of stone, re - lent, re - lent, Break, by Je - sus' cross subdued;
2. Yes! our sins have done the deed, Driv'n the nails that fixed Him there;
3. Will you let Him die in vain, Still to death pur - sue the Lord;

See His bod - y man - gled, rent, Cov - ered with His flowing blood?
Crowned with thorns His sa-cred head, Pierced Him with the cru - el spear;
O - pen, tear His wounds a - gain, Tram-ple on His pre-cious word!

Sin - ful soul, what hast thou done? Cru - ci - fied th'Incar - nate Son!
Made His soul a sac - ri - fice, For a sin - ful world He dies.
No! with all my sins I'll part, Sav - iour, take my brok-en heart.

ROCKINGHAM. L. M.

WM. COWPER, 1779.   DR. LOWELL MASON, 1832.

"JESUS IS BORN."

CALLENA LISK.　　　*CHRISTMAS HYMN.*　　　D. W. MILLER.

1. Sing, sing, ye ser - aphs white, Je - sus is born!
2. Sing, sing, ye ran - somed ones, Je - sus is born!

Past is the drear - y night, Bright is the dawn.
Hail! Sun of Right - eous - ness! Je - sus is born!

Hail! star of Beth - le - hem! Light of the proph - et's dream;
Wel - come, O Prince of Peace, Bring - ing our soul's re - lease;

Hope now doth bright - ly beam, Je - sus is born!
Bid - ding our sor - rows cease, Je - sus is born!

3 Peace and good will to men,
　Jesus is born!
Cleanse now the sinner's stain,
　Jesus is born!
Glory to God above,
For His unbounded love;
Christ shall our sins remove,
　Jesus is born!

4 Hope shines from Calvary,
　Jesus hath died!
He washed my sins away,
　Jesus hath died!
Praise to the Lamb of God,
Our reascended Lord,
By heaven and earth adored,
　Jesus is mine!

"Yea, let Him take all." 2 Sam. 19: 20.   D. W. MILLER.

1. Take my life and let it be Con - se - crat - éd, Lord, to Thee;
2. Take my voice, and let me sing Al - ways, on - ly for my King;

Take my mo-ments and my days, Let them flow in cease-less praise.
Take my lips and let them be Filled with mes - sa - ges from Thee.

Take my hands and let them move At the im-pulse of Thy love;
Take my sil - ver and my gold, Not a mite would I with-hold;

Take my feet and let them be Swift and beau - ti - ful for Thee.
Take my in - tel - lect and use Ev - 'ry power as Thou shalt choose.

3 Take my will and make it Thine,
It shall no longer be mine;
Take my heart it *is* Thine own,
It shall be Thy royal throne;
Take my love, my Lord, I pour
At Thy feet its treasure store;
Take myself, and I will be
Ever, *only*, ALL for Thee.

UNDER ORDERS.

Words arranged.

D. W. MILLER.

1. Speak, Lord, for Thy servant heareth, Speak peace to my wea - ry soul;
2. For so in the weary jour-ney O - ver life's tempest-uous sea,
3. He, who car - eth for the lil - y, And who heeds the sparrow's fall,

Help me feel that all my ways Are un - der Thy con - trol.
I know not the way I'm go - ing, But Je - sus shall pi-lot me;
Ten - der - ly shall lead His loving child, For He made and loveth all.

We know not what is ex-pe - di-ent, But we may know what is right;
I see not the rocks and quicksands, For my sight is dull and dim;
And so, when wearied and baf - fled, I know not which way to go,

And we'll never need to grope in darkness If we look to heaven for light.
But I know that Jesus is my Captain, And I take my orders from Him.
But I know that He can guide me safely, And 'tis all that I need to know.

CHORUS.

For I know that Christ my Captain is, And I take my or - ders from

Him, And I know that He will safely guide, So I take my orders from Him.

ANCHORED FAST.

Words arranged.

D. W. MILLER.

1. Toss - ing on the bil - low, Rock - ing in the blast;
2. Gone each earth - ly treas - ure, Cut a - way each mast;
3. Sor - rows mul - ti - ply - ing, Pros - pects o - ver - cast;
4. Swift - ly to my grave - bed I am mak - ing haste;

Rit. *Tempo. Refrain.*

Cling-ing to the ca - ble, I am anchored fast.
Vanished earthly pleas-ure, Still I'm anchored fast. While the tempest
Weeping, groaning, sigh-ing, Still I'm anchored fast.
Trembling 'neath the death tread, Still I'm anchored fast.

ra - ges, To the Rock of A - ges I am an-chored fast.

In ev-'ry hour spread Thy pro-tect-ing wings o'er me.
My faint-ing heart re-vive, And come and dwell in me.

On me Thy care be-stow, Thy lov-ing kind-ness show,
Au-thor of life and light, Thou hast an arm of might,

Thine arms around me throw, Show me Thy sav-ing power.
Thine is the sov-ereign right, To me Thy strength im-part.

3 Saviour, I look to Thee,
   Let me Thy fullness see;
   My wants supply,
The riches of Thy grace give me.
While at the cross I kneel
All my backslidings heal,
And my free pardon seal,
   My Saviour, hear my cry.

4 Saviour, I look to Thee,
   Thine shall the glory be;
   I know no fear,
Unfailing aid thou givest me.
On Thee my cares are laid,
On Thee my soul is staid,
Naught can my heart invade,
   My Saviour, whilst Thou'rt near.

ANTIOCH. C. M.

Arranged.

1. Joy to the world, the Lord is come. Let earth receive her King; Let
2. Joy to the earth, the Saviour reigns. Let men their songs employ; While
3. No more let sins and sorrows grow, Nor thorns infest the ground: He
4. He rules the world with truth and grace, And makes the nations prove The

ev - 'ry heart pre - pare Him room, And heav'n and nature sing, And
fields and floods, rocks, hills and plains, Re - peat the sounding joy, Re-
comes to make his bless-ings flow, Far as the curse is found, Far
glo - ries of His right-eou - ness, And wonders of His love, And

heav'n and na - ture sing, And heav'n, and heav'n and na-ture sing.
peat the sound-ing joy, Re - peat, re - peat the sounding joy.
as the curse is found, Far as, far as the curse is found.
wonders of His love, And won- ders, won - ders of His love.

TO-DAY.

L. MASON.

1. To - day the Sav-iour calls: Ye wanderers come: Oh, ye be-night-ed
2. To - day the Sav-iour calls: For ref - uge fly; The storm of vengeance

souls, Why lon - ger roam?
falls; Ru - in is nigh.

3 To-day the Saviour calls;
  Oh, listen now;
  Within these sacred walls
  To Jesus bow.

4 The Spirit calls to-day;
  Yield to His power;
  Oh, grieve Him not away,
  'Tis mercy's hour.

BATTLE SONG.

D. W. MILLER.

D. W. MILLER.

1. In bat-tle ar-ray How fearless we stand, The on-coming foe Make
2. Our Cap-tain is brave, A great conqueror, He nev-er has failed In
3. He sends us command, Only trust and obey; He'll strengthen and help. An
4. The vict'ry is ours, Thro' Christ, our great Lord, He fought the great fight, Sle

firm-er our band, For who can pre-vail 'Gainst God and His might? Hi
coun-cil or war; Im-man-uel His name, And King of all kings, An
hold us al-way; Our loins girt with truth, And faith for a shield, Th
Death with His sword, And more than all this, Our Redeemer has laid Ric

CHORUS.

sol-diers we are, Our cause is the right.
Lord of all lords, He rules o'er all things. March on, march on, march
Spir-it our sword, In bat-tle we wield.
crowns on our heads, And kings we are made.

on, march on, our Lead-er bids us ban-ish all

fear and dismay, For Christ is our Captain and Prince of our peace, Brea down the ser-ried ranks of our foes' strong ar-ray.

EVEN ME.

MRS. ELIZ. CODNER. WM. B. BRADBURY,

1. Lord, I hear of show'rs of blessing Thou art scatt'ring full and free--
2. Pass me not, O gra-cious Fa-ther! Sinful tho' my heart may be;
3. Pass me not, O ten-der Sav-iour! Let me love and cling to Thee;

Show'rs, the thirst-y land re-fresh-ing; Let some droppings fall on me—
Thou might'st leave me, but the rath-er Let Thy mer-cy fall on me—
I am long-ing for Thy fa-vor, Whilst Thou'rt calling, oh, call me—

E-ven me, e-ven me, Let Thy bless-ing fall on me.

4 Pass me not, O mighty Spirit!
Thou canst make the blind to see;
Witnesses of Jesus' merit, [me.
Speak the word of power to me-even

5 Love of God, so pure and changeless;
Blood of Christ, so rich and free;

Grace of God, so strong and boundless,
Magnify them all in me—even me.

6 Pass me not! Thy lost one bringing,
Bind my heart, O Lord, to Thee;
While the streams of life are springing,
Blessing others, oh, bless me—even me.

RESURREXIT.

Words arranged.

D. W. MILLER.

1. Lo ! the stone is rolled a - way, Death yields up his might-y prey;
2. Ev - 'ry note with rap - ture swell, And the Sav-iour's tri-umph tell;

Je - sus ris - ing from the tomb, Scat-ters all its fear-ful gloom
Where, O Death, is now thy sting? Where, thy ter-rors, vanquished king.

CHORUS.

Praise Him, ye ce - les - tial choirs, Praise and sweep your gold-en lyres;

Praise Him in the no-blest songs From ten thou - sand thousand tongues

3 Let Immanuel be adored,
Ransom, Mediator, Lord;
To creation's utmost bound
Let th' eternal praise resound.

rest, A glimpse of thy splendors un-fold, In rap-ture my soul is
cold, Where God is the life and the light, And days nev-er-more grow

blest; O Par - a-dise, when will I feel Thy waves of balm o - ver me
old; O Par - a-dise, when will I feel The bliss and the rap-ture di-

roll? With longings and yearnings my heart Looks to the home of my soul.
vine? When ent'ring the beau-ti-ful gate, I'll know all Thy joys are mine.

3 O Paradise, Paradise fair,
    I'll sing of thee while I roam;
  My soul has its treasure most rare,
    O land of my love, my home.
  O Paradise, full well I know
    The world is as naught to compare
  With thee, land of purest delight,
    For One who loves me is there.

ZERAH.

L. MASON.

1. While shepherds watched their flocks by night All seat-ed on the groun
2. "Fear not," said He—for might-y dread Had siezed their troubled mind-

The an - gel of the Lord came down And glo - ry shone a-round,
"Glad tid - ings of great joy I bring To you and all man-kind,

The an - gel of the Lord came down And glo-ry shone a - round.
"Glad tid - ings of great joy I bring To you and all mankind."

3 "To you, in David's town, this day,
Is born of David's line,
‖: The Saviour, who is Christ, the Lord;
And this shall be the sign. :‖

4 "The heavenly Babe you there shall
To human view displayed, [find
‖: All meanly wrapped in swathing
And in a manger laid." :‖ [bands,

5 Thus spake the seraph, and forthwith
Appeared a shining throng
‖: Of angels, praising God, and thus
Addressed their joyful song. :‖

6 "All glory be to God on high,
And to the earth be peace;
‖: Good will henceforth from heaven to
Begin and never cease. :‖ [man,

———

1 O, for a thousand tongues to sing
My great Redeemer's praise.
‖: The glories of my God and King,
The triumphs of His grace. :‖

2 My gracious Master, and my God,
Assist me to proclaim,
‖: To spread through all the earth abroa
The honors of Thy name. :‖

3 Jesus, the name that charms our fears
That bids our sorrows cease;
‖: 'Tis music in the sinner's ears,
'Tis life, and health, and peace. :‖

4 He cancels all the power of sin,
He sets the prisoner free;
‖: His blood can make the foulest clean
His blood availed for me. :‖

5 He speaks, and listening to His voice
New life the dead receive;
‖: The mournful, broken heart rejoice,
The humble poor believe. :‖

6 Hear Him, ye deaf, his praise, ye dumb
Your loosened tongues employ;
‖: Ye blind, behold your Saviour come
And leap, ye lame, for joy. :‖

WESLEY, 1740.

1. Stay ! wea - ry sin - ner, bur-dened one,   O where-fore toil you
2. Yes ! when He, from His loft - y throne, Stooped down to do and

so?   Cease now your do-ing; all was done,   Yes ! long, long a-
die,   Then ev - 'ry thing was ful - ly done;   Oh, hearken to His

CHORUS.

go.   And nothing, eith - er great or small,   Remains for you to
cry.

do;   For Je - sus died and paid it all   A long while a - go.

3 And till to Jesus' work you cling,
    Just by a simple faith,
All "doing" is a deadly thing,
    For "doing" ends in death.

4 Then cast your deadly "doing"
    All down at Jesus' feet,
And stand in Him, in Him alone,
    All glorious and complete.

HOSANNA. C. M.

D. W. MILLER.

1. Ho - san - na to the Prince of light, Who clothed him - self with clay, En - tered the i - ron gates of death, And tore the bars a - way, And tore the bars a - way.

2. Death is no more the king of dread, Since our Im - man - uel rose; He took the ty - rant's sting a - way, And spoiled our hell - ish foes, And spoiled our hellish foes.

3. See how the Con - qu'ror mounts a - loft, And to His Fa - ther flies, With scars of hon - or in His flesh, And triumph in His eyes, And tri-umph in His eyes.

4 There our exalted Saviour reigns,
And scatters blessings down;
Our Jesus fills the middle seat
Of the celestial throne.

5 Raise your devotion, mortal tongues,
To reach His blest abode;
Sweet be the accents of your song
To our incarnate God.

6 Bright angels, strike your loudest
Your sweetest voices raise; [strings,
Let heaven, and all created things,
Sound our Immanuel's praise.

---

1 Hark to the trump! behold it breaks
The sleep of ages now;
And lo! the light of glory shines
On many an aching brow.

2 Changed in a moment, full of life,
The quick, the dead, arise,
Responsive to the angel's voice
That calls us to the skies.

3 Ascending through the clouds of air,
On eagle wings we soar,
To dwell in the full joy of love,
And sorrow there no more.

4 O Lord, the bright and blessed hope,
That cheered us through the past,
Of full, eternal rest in Thee,
Is all fulfilled at last.

5 Past conflict now, O Lord, 'tis ours
Through everlasting days,
To sing our song of victory
To Thine eternal praise.

Words arr.   "I came not to call the righteous, but sinners."   D. W. MILLER.

1. Come, ye wea-ry, heavy-lad en, Lost and ru-ined by the fall; If you

tar - ry till you're bet-ter You will nev - er come at all. Hear the

Refrain.

bless - ed in - vi - ta -tion, Sinners, Je - sus came to call; Not the

right-eous, not the righteous, But to sin - ners is the call.

Let not conscience make you linger,
  Nor of fitness proudly dream;
All the fitness He requireth,
  Is to feel your need of Him.

3 Your Redeemer, now ascended,
  Pleads the merits of His blood;
Venture on Him, venture wholly,
  Let no other trust intrude.

D. W. MILLER.

1. Ho, ev-'ry one that thirsts! draw nigh; 'Tis God invites a fall-en
2. Come to the liv-ing wa-ters,come;Sinner's,o-bey your Master'

race;Mer-cy and free sal-va-tion buy, Buy wine,and milk,and gospe
call; Re-turn, ye wea-ry wand'rers,home,And find my grace is free fo

grace. Nothing ye in exchange shall give,Leave all you have and all b
all. Nothing ye in exchange shall give,Leave all you have and all b

hind;Freely the gift of God receive,Pardon and peace in Jesus find.
hind;Freely the gift of God receive,Pardon and peace in Jesus find·

1 As pants the hart for water-brooks,
So pants my soul, O God, for Thee;
For Thee it thirsts, to Thee it looks,
And longs the living God to see.
Oh, why art thou cast down,my soul?
And what should so disquiet thee?
Still hope in God, and Him extol,[me.
Whose face brings saving health to

2 Deep calls to deep in thunder loud,
Thy water-spouts repeat the call;
Whilst o'er me roll the billows proud
And all thy waves upon me fall.
Yet shall the Lord command by day
His loving-kindness; and His song
By night be with me; and I'll pray
To Him who doth my life prolong

D. W. MILLER.

1. There were ninety and nine that safely lay   In the shel-ter of the
2. "Yet Lord, Thou hast here Thy ninety and nine, Are they not enough for
3. "Lord, whence are those blood tracks all the way, That mark out the mountain's
4. But none of the ransomed ev-er knew How deep were the waters

fold;   But   one was   out   on   the   hills   a - way,   Far
Thee?" But the   shep-herd made   an-swer, "'Tis one of mine   Has
track?" "They   were shed for   one   who   went a - stray,   Ere the
crossed;   Nor how dark was the night that the Lord passed thro'   Ere He

off from the gates of gold.   A - way on the mountains, wild and bare, A-
wandered a - way from me."   And although the road be rough and steep, I
shepherd could bring him back." "Lord, whence are Thy hands so rent and torn?"
                                                          'They're
found His sheep that was lost. Far out   in the des-ert, heard He its cry, Sick,

Refrain.

Work while the dew is spark - ling, Work 'mid spring-ing flowers;
Fill bright - est hours with la - bor, Rest comes sure and soon.

Work when the day grows bright-er, Work in the glow-ing sun;
Give ev - 'ry fly - ing min - ute Something to keep in store;

Work, for the night is com - ing, When man's work is done.
Work, for the night is com - ing. When man works no more.

3 Work, for the night is coming,
Under the sunset skies;
While their bright tints are glowing,
Work, for the daylight flies;
Work till the last beam fadeth,
Fadeth to shine no more;
Work while the night is dark'ning,
When man's work is o'er.

I BRING MY SINS TO THEE.

FRANCIS. R. HAVERGAL. Arr.   D. W. MILLER.

1. I bring my sins to Thee, The sins I can - not count,
2. My heart to Thee I bring, The heart I can - not read;
3. I bring my griefs to Thee, The griefs I can - not tell;

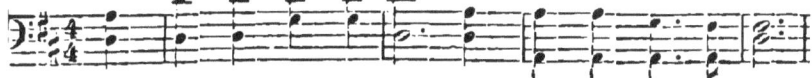

That I may cleans - ed be In Thy once o - pen'd fount;
A faith - less, wand'ring thing, An e - vil heart, in - deed;
No words shall need - ed be, Thou know-est all too well.

I bring them, Sav - iour, all to Thee, The bur - den is too
I bring it, Sav - iour. now to Thee, That fixed and faith - ful
I bring the sor - row laid on me, O suf - fering Sav-iour,

great for me; I bring my sins to Thee, My Sav-iour, all to Thee.
it may be; I bring my heart to Thee, My Sav-iour, now to Thee.
all to Thee; I bring my griefs to Thee, My Sav-iour, all to Thee.

My joys to Thee I bring,
The joys Thy love has given,
That each may be a wing
To lift me nearer heaven.
bring them, Saviour, all to Thee,
Who hast procured them all for me;
bring my joys to Thee,
My Saviour, all to Thee.

5 My life I bring to Thee,
I would not be my own,
O Saviour, let me be
Thine ever. Thine alone.
My heart, my life, my all I bring
To Thee, my Saviour and my King,
My life I bring to Thee,
My Saviour, all to Thee.

1. Je - sus shall reign where'er the sun Does his suc - cess - ive
2. To Him shall end - less prayer be made And end - less prais - es

jour - neys run; His king - dom spread from shore to shore, Till
crown His head; His name like sweet per - fume shall rise With

moons shall wax and wane no more. From north to south the princ - es meet
ev - 'ry morn - ing sac - ri - fice. Peo - ple and realms of ev - 'ry tongue

To pay their homage at His feet; While west - ern em - pires
Dwell on His love with sweetest song, And in - fant voic - es

own their Lord, And sav - age tribes at - tend His word.
shall pro - claim Their ear - ly bless - ings on His name.

D. W. MILLER.

1. Once I tho't my mountain strong, Firm - ly fix'd no more to move;
2. Lit - tle, then, myself I knew, Lit - tle thought of Sa - tan's pow'r;
3. Sav-iour! shine, and cheer my soul, Bid my dy - ing hopes re - vive,

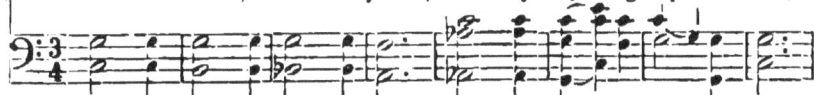

Then my Sav-iour was my song, Then my soul was filled with love:
Now I feel my sins re - new, Now I feel the storm-y hour:
Make my wounded spir - it whole, Far a - way the tempt - er drive;

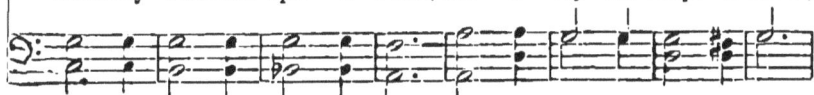

Those were golden, hap - py days, Sweetly spent in pray'r and praise.
Sin has put my joys to flight, Sin has turn'd my day to night.
Speak the word, and set me free. Let me live a - lone to Thee.

1 Go to dark Gethsemane,
Ye who feel the tempter's power;
Your Redeemer's conflict see;
Watch with Him one bitter hour;
Turn not from His griefs away,
Learn of Jesus Christ to pray.

2 Follow to the judgment-hall,
View the Lord of life arraign'd:
Oh, the wormwood and the gall!
Oh, the pangs His soul sustained!
Shun not suffering, shame, or loss;
Learn of Him to bear the cross.

3 Calvary's mournful mountain climb:
There, adoring at His feet,
Mark that miracle of time,
God's own sacrifice complete:
"It is finished," hear Him cry;
Learn of Jesus Christ to die.

4 Early hasten to the tomb,
Where they laid His breathless clay;
All is solitude and gloom;
Who hath taken Him away?
Christ has ris'n, He meets our eyes,
Saviour, teach us how to rise.

1 Rock of ages! cleft for me!
Let me hide myself in Thee:
Let the water and the blood,
From Thy wounded side which flowed,
Be of sin the double cure;
Cleanse me from its guilt and power.

2 Not the labor of my hands
Can fulfill the law's demands;
Could my zeal no respite know,
Could my tears forever flow,
All for sin could not atone,
Thou must save, and Thou alone.

3 Nothing in my hand I bring,
Simply to Thy cross I cling;
Naked, come to Thee for dress,
Helpless, look to Thee for grace;
Vile, I to the fountain fly,
Wash me, Saviour, or I die.

4 While I draw this fleeting breath,
When my heart-strings break in death,
When I soar to worlds unknown,
See Thee on Thy judgment-throne,
Rock of ages, cleft for me,
Let me hide myself in Thee.

Words arranged. D. W. MILLER.

Boys.

1. Dear lit - tle singing bird out in the tree, Singing so light-ly and
2. Dear lit - tle hon-ey-bee, searching for sweet, Loading with pollen your
3. Dear lit - tle lil - y - bell, spotless and white, Rooted in earth, and yet

seem - ing so free; What is the les - son you're teaching to me?
deft lit - tle feet; Have you some les - sons for trou-bled souls meet?
drink-ing heav'ns light, Can my heart be like you, so pure and bright?

Girls.

Trust and sing, trust and sing, Keep all day on the wing; And, when night shadows
Trust and try, trust and try, 'Tis the drones that must die; So in morning or
Trust and love, trust and love, Keep your eyes fixed above; And thro' shower and

All.

gath - er, just sing, trust and sing; Trust and sing, trust and sing.
eve - ning, just try, trust and try; Trust and try, trust and try.
sun-shine, still love, trust and love; Trust and love, trust and love.

4 Dear meek forget-me-not, tender and true,
Love in thy beaming eye, hope in thy hue,
What is the lesson to mortals from you?
Trust and pray, trust and pray,
From thyself look away;
And tho' tempests may threaten, still pray, trust and pray;
Trust and pray, trust and pray.

1. Around the throne of God in heaven Thousands of children stand, Chil-

dren whose sins are all forgiv'n, A ho - ly, hap - py

band, Singing glo - ry, glo - ry, glo - ry be to God on high.

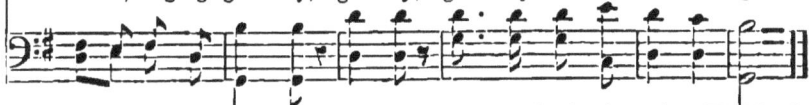

2 In flowing robes of spotless white,
  See every one arrayed,
Dwelling in everlasting light,
And joys that never fade.—*Cho.*

3 What bro't them to that world above,
  That heaven so bright and fair,
Where all is peace, and joy, and love,
How came those children there?—*Cho.*

4 Because the Saviour shed His blood
  To wash away their sin,
Bathed in that pure and precious flood,
Behold them white and clean.—*Cho.*

5 On earth they sought the Saviour's grace,
  On earth they lov'd His name;
So now they see His blessed face,
And stand before the Lamb.—*Cho.*

LABAN. S. M.

GEO. HEATH, 1781.   DR. LOWELL MASON, 1830.

1. My soul, be on thy guard, Ten thou-sand foes a - rise;
2. O watch, and fight, and pray; The bat - tle ne'er give o'er;
3. Ne'er thihk the vic - t'ry won, Nor lay thine ar - mor down;

1. Lit - tle drops of dew, They are ver - y small; In the qui - et night
2. Lit - tle drops of dew, They are ver - y still; Without an - y noise

On the flow'rs they fall, On the blades of grass, On each ten - der spra
They their course ful-fill: Si - lent - ly they come, Si - lent - ly they go;

Mak-ing all so fresh For the com-ing day. Lit - tle drops of dew,
Not by words, but deeds We their val - ue know. Lit - tle drops of dew,
3. Lit - tle girls and boys,

They are ver - y bright; Just like ti - ny pearls Are they to the sight;
They are ver - y meek; No reward they ask, No ap-plause they seek;
Tell us, should not you Strive from day to day To be like the dew?

Wear - ing all the hues Of a spark - ling gem,
With - out thought of gain, They de - light to cheer
Gen - tle, hum - ble, kind, Do - ing your small part

For tho sun-beams rest Lov-ing-ly on them.
Thirst-y buds and flowers Through-out all the year.
In this might-y world, With a will-ing heart.

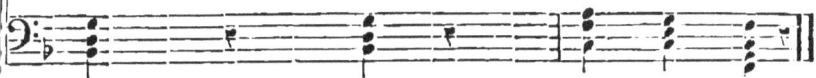

I THINK WHEN I READ THAT SWEET STORY.

Arr. by D. W. MILLER.

1. I think when I read that sweet sto-ry of old, When Je-sus was here among men, How He called little chil-dren as lambs to His fold; I should like to have been with Him then.

2. I wish that His hands had been placed on my head, That His arms had been thrown around me, And that I might have seen His kind look when He said, "Let the lit-tle ones come un-to me."

3. Yet still to His foot-stool in pray'r I may go, And ask for a share in His love; And if I thus earn-est-ly seek Him be-low, I shall see Him and hear Him a-bove.

4 In that beautiful place He is gone to prepare
For all who are washed and forgiven;
And many dear children are gathering there,
For of such is the kingdom of heaven.

5 I long for the joys of that glorious time,
The sweetest, and brightest, and best;
When the dear little children of every clime,
Shall crowd to His arms and be blest.

DELAY NOT. 11s.

D. W. MILLER.

1. De - lay not, de-lay not, oh sin-ner, draw near; The wa-ters of
2. De - lay not, de-lay not; why long-er a-buse The love and com
3. De - lay not, de-lay not, oh sin - ner, to come, For mer-cy stil
4. De - lay not, de-lay not—the Spir-it of grace, Long griev'd and re-

life are now flow - ing for thee: No price is de-mand-ed, the
pas-sion of Je - sus thy God? A fount-ain is o-pened, ho'
lin - gers, and calls thee to - day, Her voice is not heard in the
sist - ed, may take its sad flight, And leave thee in darkness to

Sav - iour is here, Redemption is pur-chased, sal-va - tion is free.
canst thou re - fuse To wash and be cleansed in His par - don-ing blood.
vale of the tomb; Her message, unheed - ed, will soon pass a - way.
fin - ish thy race—To sink in the gloom of e - ter - ni-ty's night.

1 Acquaint thyself quickly, oh sinner, with God,
And joy like the sunshine shall beam on the road.
And peace like the dew-drops shall fall on thy head,
And sleep like an angel shall visit thy bed.

2 Acquaint thyself quickly, oh sinner, with God.
And He shall be with thee when fears are abroad;
Thy safeguard in dangers that threaten thy path,
Thy joy in the valley and shadow of death.

1 Oh turn ye, oh turn ye, for why will ye die?
Since God in His mercy is coming so nigh,
Since Jesus invites you, the Spirit says, come,
And angels are waiting to welcome you home.

2 How vain the delusion, that while you delay,
Your hearts may grow better, your chains melt away:
Come wretched, come guilty, come just as you are;
All helpless and dying, to Jesus repair.

3 The contrite in heart He will freely receive;
Oh, why will you not the glad message believe?
If sin be your burden, oh, will you not come?
'Tis you He makes welcome; He bids you come home.

M. L. H.   D. W. MILLER.

1. Treas - ures in heav'n laid up a - bove,
2. Treas - ures in heav'n, how blest the thought,

An in - t'rest in a Re - deem - er's love;
By the gold of earth they can ne'er be bought;

The pearl of price ex - ceed - ing great,
These gems shall shine with bright - 'ning ray

A crown of glo - ry and robes of state.
When the pomp of earth has passed a - way.

3 Treasures in heaven, secure them now,
  While the bloom of youth is on your brow;
  While grace holds out, with wondrous love,
  The righest gifts of the world above.

4 Treasures in heaven, then ne'er delay
  To make them yours while yet you may,
  While Jesus sweetly bids you come,
  Oh, gather them to your joyful home.

ARISE, MY SOUL. H. M.

D. W. MILLER.

A - rise, my soul, a - rise, Shake off thy guilt-y fears; A bleeding sacri-

fice In thy be-half ap-pears. Before the throne my Surety stands, B

fore the throne my Surety stands; My name is writ - ten on His hands.

1 Arise, my soul, arise,
  Shake off thy guilty fears;
A bleeding sacrifice
  In thy behalf appears.
Before the throne my Surety stands;
My name is written on His hands.

2 Five bleeding wounds He bears,
  Received on Calvary:
They pour effectual prayers,
  They strongly speak for me:
Forgive him, oh, forgive, they cry,
Nor let that ransomed sinner die.

3 The Father hears him pray,
  His dear annointed One;
He can not turn away
  The presence of His Son:
His Spirit answers to the blood,
And tells me I am born of God.

1 Ye tribes of Adam, join
  With heav'n, and earth, and seas,
And offer notes divine
  To your Creator's praise.
Ye holy throng of angels bright,
In worlds of light, begin the song.

2 Thou sun with dazzling rays,
  And moon that rules the night,
Shine to your Maker's praise
  With stars of twinkling light.
His power declare, ye floods on high,
And clouds that fly in empty air.

3 The shining worlds above
  In glorious order stand,
Or in swift courses move
  By his supreme command.
He spake the word, and all their fram
From nothing came to praise the Lor

OH, HOW HAPPY ARE THEY.

C. WESLEY. Arr. by D. W. MILLER.

1. Oh, how hap-py are they, Who the Sav-iour o-bey,
2. That sweet com-fort was mine, When the fa-vor di-vine
3. 'Twas a heav-en be-low My Re-deem-er to know,

And have laid up their treas-ure a-bove; Tongue can nev-er ex-
I re-ceived thro' the blood of the Lamb; When my heart first be-
And the an-gels could do noth-ing more, Than to fall at His

press The sweet com-fort and peace Of a soul in its
lieved, What a joy I re-ceived, What a heav-en in
feet, And the sto-ry re-peat, And the Lov-er of

ear-li-est love, Of a soul in its ear-li-est love.
Je-sus' sweet name, What a heav-en in Je-sus' sweet name.
sin-ners a-dore, And the Lov-er of sin-ners a-dore.

4 Jesus all the day long
   Was my joy and my song;
Oh, that all His salvation might see;
   He hath loved me, I cried,
   He hath suffered and died,
To redeem even rebels like me.

5 Oh, the rapturous height
   Of that holy delight,
Which I felt in the life-giving blood;
   Of my Saviour possessed,
   I was perfectly blessed,
As if filled with the fullness of God.

JESUS, LOVER OF MY SOUL.

D. W. MILLER.

1. Je - sus, lov - er of my soul, Let me to Thy bo - som
2. Oth - er ref - uge have I none, Hangs my help-less soul on

fly; While the near - er wa - ters roll, While the tempest still is
Thee; Leave, oh, leave me not a - lone, Still support and com-fort

high, Hide me, O my Sav-iour, hide, Till the storm of life is past;
me. All my trust on Thee is stayed, All my help from Thee I bring;

Rall.

Safe in - to the ha - ven guide, Oh, re - ceive my soul at last.
Cov - er my de - fense-less head With the shad - ow of Thy wing.

3 Thou, O Christ, art all I want,
  All in all in Thee I find;
Raise the fallen, cheer the faint,
  Heal the sick, and lead the blind;
Just and holy is Thy name,
  I am all unrighteousness;
Vile and full of sin I am,
  Thou art full of truth and grace.

4 Plenteous grace with Thee is found,
  Grace to cover all my sin;
Let the healing streams abound,
  Make and keep me pure within;
Thou of life the fountain art,
  Freely let me take of Thee;
Spring Thou up within my heart,
  Rise to all eternity.

D. W. MILLER.

Slowly.

1. Depth of mer - cy, can there be   Mer - cy still   reserved for   me?
2. There for me the Saviour stands, Shows His wounds and spreads His hands;

Can   my God His wrath for - bear, Me,   the chief of sin - ners, spare?
Je - sus, an - swer from a - bove, Is   not all Thy na - ture love?

I   have long withstood His   grace, Long provoked Him face to face;
Now in - cline me to   re - pent, Let   me now my sins   la-ment;

Would not heark - en to   His   call. Grieved Him by a thousand falls.
Now my foul re - volt de - plore, Weep, believe, and sin no   more.

Refrain.

Je - sus weeps, He loves me   still, Je - sus weeps and loves me still.

SWEET THE MOMENTS.

D. W. MILLER.

1. Sweet the moments, rich in bless - ing, Which before the cross I spend;
2. Here I'll sit for - ev - er view - ing Mer - cy streaming in His blood

Life, and health, and peace possess - ing, From the sinner's dy-ing Friend.
Precious drops my soul be-dew - ing, Plead and claim my peace with God,

Tru - ly bless-ed is this sta - tion, Low be - fore His cross to lie;
Here it is I find my heav - en, While up-on the cross I gaze;

While I see di - vine compas - sion Floating in His lan-guid eye.
Love I much? I'm much for-giv - en, I'm a mir - a - cle of grace.

1 Jesus, full of all compassion,
Hear Thy humble suppliant's cry;
Let me know Thy great salvation;
See, I languish, faint, and die.
Guilty, but with heart relenting,
Overwhelmed with helpless grief,
Prostrate at Thy feet repenting—
Send, oh, send me quick relief.

2 Whither should a wretch be flying,
But to Him who comfort gives?
Whither, from the dread of dying,
But to Him who ever lives?
While I view Thee, wounded, grieving
Breathless on th'accursed tree,
Fain I'd feel my heart believing
Thou didst suffer thus for me.

LORD, REMEMBER ME.

Words arrranged. D. W. MILLER.

1 Je - sus, Thou art the sin - ner's friend, Lord, re - mem - ber me;
2. Lov - ing Sav - iour, hear my cry, Lord, re - mem - ber me;

Let Thy grace on me de - scend, Lord, re - mem - ber me;
Trembling, to Thy arms I fly, Lord, re - mem - ber me;

I am guilt - y, I am vile, Lord, re - mem - ber me;
I have sinned, but Thou hast died, Lord, re - mem - ber me;

Send me one compassionate smile, Lord, re - mem - ber me.
In Thy mer - cy let me hide, Lord, re - mem - ber me.

3 Though I perish I will pray,
  Lord, remember me;
Thou art life, the living way,
  Lord, remember me.
Thou hast said Thy grace is free,
  Lord, remember me;
Have compassion, Lord, on me,
  Lord, remember me.

4 To the cross my all I bring,
  Lord, remember me;
By my faith to Thee I cling,
  Lord, remember me.
Wash me in that cleansing flood,
  Lord, remember me;
And renew me in Thy blood,
  Lord, remember me.

ARMY OF THE LORD.

G. K. MARINER.   D. W. MILLER.

1. Come, ye children, join the ar - - - my, Ar-my of . . . the liv-i

1. Come, ye chil - dren, join the Ar - my, Ar-my of the

Lord;   He in - vites you, He in - vites . . . you By H

liv - ing Lord; He in - vites you, He in - vites you,

spir - - - - - it through His word,

By His spir - it thro' His word. Come, we have a

glo - rious Leader, One who will most faithful prove; He is might-

wise, and val - iant, O'er us is His ban - ner, love,

He is might-y, wise, and val-iant, O'er us is His ban-ner, love.

2 We are marching, marching, marching,
  Marching up the shining way,
To a city light and blissful,
  To the realms of endless day,
Where our warfare will be over,
  Cares and fears we'll have no more,
‖: Where we'll camp with Christ forever,
  And have joy forevermore. :‖

3 Then put on the Christian's armor,
  Fall ye in the ranks, fall in;
Forward march, march on like heroes,
  Fighting satan, self, and sin.
Though their forces are like legion,
  And their ramparts high and strong,
‖: And their fiery darts fall 'round you,
  Steady, forward, march along.:‖

4 Look to Jesus, perfect Leader,
  In Him let your heart be strong;
Though the battle's long and fearful,
  You shall sing the victor's song.
"Glory, honor to our Saviour,
  We have conquered through His blood,"
‖: You shall rest with Him forever,
  In His heavenly abode. :‖

5 One and all, come, join this army,
  Army of the living Lord;
He invites you, He invites you,
  By His spirit through His word.
Come, we're marching on to glory,
  Glory on the "shining shore,"
‖: In our Saviour's blessed mansions,
  Where we'll dwell forevermore. :‖

BE IN EARNEST.

D. W. MILLER.

1. Time is earn-est, pass-ing by, Death is earn-est, drawing nigh,
2. Heav'n is earn-est; sol-emn-ly Float its voic-es down to thee,

Sin-ner, wilt thou trif-ling be? Time and death ap-peal to thee.
O thou mor-tal, art thou gay, Sport-ing thro' thine earth-ly day?

Life is earn-est, when 'tis o'er, Thou re-turn-est nev-er-more;
God is earn-est, kneel and pray, Ere thy sea-son pass a-way;

Soon to meet e-ter-ni-ty: Wilt thou nev-er earn-est be?
Ere be set His judgment throne, Vengeance read-y, mer-cy gone!

3 Christ is earnest, bids thee come,
Paid thy spirit's priceless sum;
Wilt thou spurn thy Saviour's love,
Pleading with thee from above?
Art thou earnest? wretched one,
That despiseth God's dear Son!
Madness! dying sinner, turn,
Lest His wrath upon thee burn.

4 When thy pleasures all depart,
What will soothe thy fainting heart,
Friendless, desolate, alone,
Entering a world unknown?
Oh, be in earnest, see thy fate,
Wait not, lest it be too late ;
Stay no longer, rise and flee;
Lo! thy Saviour waits for thee.

Rev. A. E. TAYLOR.   D. W. MILLER.

1. I'll have no fear of dy - ing, Did He not die? On

Je - sus' grace re - ly - ing, No doubts my calm heart

try - ing, Se - rene I'll die, Se - rene I'll die.

2 Where is the sting of dying
    If thus I die?
  My soul in peace relying,
  On Him all satisfying,
    With Christ so nigh,
    With Christ so nigh.

4 Why should I shrink from dying,
    When thus I die?
  My faith its watchword crying,
  My love with banner flying,
    In victory,
    in victory.

5 From earth to heaven is dying,
    I joy to die;
  The blissful comforts nighing,
  The light and glories spying,
    I mount on high,
    I mount on high.

6 My Saviour comes in dying,
    In Him I die; .
  With His soft call complying,
  On His warm bosom lying,
    To live I die,
    To live I die.

ALL HAIL THE GLORIOUS MORN.

D. W. MILLER.

1. All hail the glo - rious morn That saw our Sav - iour rise, Wit
2. The con - quer - or as - scends In tri - umph to the skies; Ce
3. Yes, the Re - deem - er rose, The Sav - iour left the dead. And

vic-t'ry bright adorned. And triumph in His eyes; Ye saints, ex - tol yo
les - tial hosts at-tend To crown His vic - to ries; Hark! they proclaimH
o'er our hell-ish foes High raised His conqu'ring head; In wild dismay tl

ris - en Lord, And sing His praise with sweet accord, Ye Saints.ex-
glo-rious name. And heav'n resounds Immanuel's fame; Hark! they pro-
guards around Fall to the ground, and sink a - way; In wild dis-

tol your ris - en Lord, And sing His praise with sweet accord.
claim His glo-rious name, And heav'n resounds Im - man - uel's fame.
may the guards a-round Fall to the ground, and sink a-way.

1 Lo! the angelic bands
In full assembly meet,
To wait His high commands,
And worship at His feet;
|: Joyful they come, And win their way
From realms of day To Jesus' tomb.:||

2 Then back to heaven they fly,
And the glad tidings bear:
Hark! as they soar on high,
What music fills the air:
|: Their anthems say, "Jesus who bled,
Hath left the dead; He rose to-day.":||

3 Ye mortals, catch the sound,
Redeemed by Him from hell;
And send the echo round
The globe on which you dwell;
|: Transported cry, "Jesus who bled,
Hath left the dead, No more to die."

4 All hail! triumphant Lord!
Who saved us with Thy blood!
Wide be Thy name adored,
Thou rising, reigning God!
|: With thee we rise, With thee we reigi
And empires gain, Beyond the skies.

D. W. MILLER.   D. W. MILLER.

1. God so lov-ed the world in its sin-ful es-tate,
2. And His pre-cious blood flowed on the cross when He died,
3. And He con-quered grim Death, That to men He might give

That He sent His dear Son full a-tone-ment to make.
And it cleans-es the sins of the world in its tide.
Life e-ter-nal to all that on Him do be-lieve.

CHORUS.

Hal-le-lu-jah and glo-ry to the Lamb that was

slain, Who has borne all our sins, and has cleansed ev'ry stain.

4 And the promise He sealed with His blood, and is sure,
  And His Spirit bears witness, 'twill always endure.—*Cho.*

5 Now will he that believes have a treasure within,
  And the Saviour will rescue when tempted to sin.—*Cho.*

6 And forever in heaven a glorious throng
  Of redeemed ones will praise Him, and sing the new song.—*Cho.*

NEARER, MY GOD. 6s & 4s.

Arr. by D. W. MILLER.

1. Near - er, my God, to Thee, Near - er to Thee!
2. Though like a wan - der - er, The sun gone down,
3. There let the way ap - pear, Steps up to heav'n;

E'en tho' it be a cross That rais - eth me! Still all my
Dark - ness be o - ver me, My rest a stone, Yet in my
All that Thou send-est me, In mer - cy giv'n; An - gels to

song shall be, Near - er, my God, to Thee, Near - er, my
dreams I'd be, Near - er, my God, to Thee, Near - er, my
beck - on me Near - er, my God, to Thee, Near - er, my

God, to Thee.
God, to Thee. Near - er, my God, to Thee, Near - er to Thee.
God, to Thee.

4 Then, with my waking thoughts,
Bright with Thy praise,
Out of my stony griefs
Bethel I'll raise;
So by my woes to be,
Nearer, my God to Thee,
Nearer to Thee.

5 Or, if on joyful wing,
Cleaving the sky,
Sun, moon, and stars forgot,
Upward I fly,
Still all my song shall be,
Nearer, my God, to Thee,
Nearer to Thee.

CAST THY BURDEN ON THE LORD.   99

Arr. by D. W. MILLER.

Cast thy bur-den on the Lord, On-ly lean up-on His word; Thou wilt soon have cause to bless His e-ter-nal faith-ful-ness.

1 Cast thy burden on the Lord,
Only lean upon His word;
Thou wilt soon have cause to bless
His eternal faithfulness.

2 He sustains thee by His hand,
He enables thee to stand;
Those whom Jesus once hath loved,
From His grace are never moved.

3 Heaven and earth may pass away,
God's free grace shall not decay;
He has promised to fulfill
All the pleasure of His will.

4 Jesus! guardian of Thy flock,
Be Thyself our constant Rock;
Make us by Thy powerful hand
Strong as Zion's mountain stand.

1 Wait, my soul, upon the Lord,
To His gracious promise flee,
Laying hold upon His word:
"As thy days thy strength shall be."

2 If the sorrows of thy case
Seem peculiar still to thee,
God has promised needful grace:
"As thy days thy strength shall be."

3 Days of trial, days of grief,
In succession thou mayst see:
This is still thy sweet belief;
"As thy days thy strength shall be."

4 Through all time I am secure,
With Thy promise, full and free,
Ever faithful, ever sure,
"As thy days thy strength shall be."

YES, FOR ME.

D. W. MILLER.

D. W. MILLER.

1. Yes, for me, for me my Sav - iour Came from heav'n to
2. Yes, for me, for me He car - eth, Gives me grace, dis-
3. Yes, for me, for me He suf - fered, Suf - fered all the

earth be - low, Sought me when I was a stran - ger,
pels my fears; Yes, with me, with me He shar - eth
ag - o - ny; And for me made full a - tone - ment,

Refrain.

All be - cause He loved me so.
All my sor - rows, All my tears. Yes, for me,
That from sin I might be free.

yes, for me, All be - cause He loved me so.

4 Yes, for me He ever pleadeth
   At the Father's mercy-seat,
Yes, for me He intercedeth,
   Never ceasing in His love.

5 Yes, in me His fullness dwelleth,
   For into my heart He came;
Mine is joy above the angels,
   Sing I my Redeemer's fame.

D. W. MILLER.

1. I lay my sins on Je - sus, The spot - less Lamb of God;

He bears them all. and frees us From the ac - curs - ed load;

I bring my guilt to Je - sus To wash my crim-son stains

White in His blood most precious, Till not a spot re - mains.

2 I lay my wants on Jesus,
    All fullness dwells in Him;
He heals all my diseases,
    He doth my soul redeem.
I lay my griefs on Jesus,
    My burdens and my cares;
He from them all releases,
    He all my sorrows shares.

3 I long to be like Jesus,
    Meek. loving. lowly, mild;
I long to be like Jesus,
    The Father's holy child.
I long to be with Jesus,
    Amid the heavenly throng.
To sing with saints His praises,
    To learn the angels' song.

Words arranged.

1. Stand up, stand up for Je-sus, Ye sol-diers
2. Stand up, stand up for Je-sus, Stand in His st

high His roy-al ban-ner, It must not suf
arm of flesh will fail you, Ye dare not trus

vic-t'ry un-to vic-t'ry His ar-my sha
on the gos-pel ar-mor, And watching un

ev-'ry foe is van-quished, Christ is Lord
du-ty calls, or dan-ger, Be not war

up, stand up for Je-sus, The trum-
up, stand up for Je-sus, The strife

bey, Forth to the might - y con - flict On this glo - rious
long, This day the noise of bat - tle, Then the vic - tor's

day; "Ye that are men, now serveHim," 'Gainst a host of
song; For him that o - . ver-com - eth, Crowns of life shall

foes, Your cour - age rise with dan-ger, Strength to strength oppose.
be, He with the King of glo - ry Reigns e - ter - nal - ly.

CHILD OF SIN.

HASTINGS.

1. { Child of sin . and sor - row, Filled with dis - may, }
   { Wait not for to - mor - row, Yield thee to - day; }
2. { Child of sin and sor - row, Why wilt thou die? }
   { Come while thou canst bor - row Help from on high: }

Child of sin and sor - row, Hear and o - bey.
Child of sin and sor - row, Would bring thee nigh.

NOT WORTHY, LORD.

D. W. MILLER.

1. Not wor-thy, Lord, to gath-er up the crumbs, With trembling
2. One word from Thee, my Lord, one smile, one look, And I could
3. I hear Thy voice, Thou bidst me come and rest; I come, I

hand, that from Thy ta - ble fall, A wea - ry, heav - y-
face the cold, rough world a - gain, And with that treas - ure
kneel, I clasp Thy pierc - ed feet; Thou bidst me take my

la - den sin-ner comes To plead Thy prom-ise, and o - bey Thy
in my heart could brook The wrath of dev - ils, and the scorn of
place a welcome guest A - mong Thy saints, and of Thy banquet

call; I am not wor - thy to be called Thy child, Nor sit the
men; And is not mer - cy Thy pre - rog - a - tive— Free mer - cy,
eat; My praise can on - ly breathe it-self in pray'r, My pray'r can

last and low - est at Thy board; Too long a wan - d'rer
bound - less, fath - om - less, di - vine? Me, Lord, the chief of
on - ly lose it - self in Thee; Dwell Thou for - ev - er

and too oft be-guiled, I on-ly ask one rec-on-cil-ing word.
sin-ners, me for-give, And Thine, the greater glo-ry, on-ly Thine.
in my heart, and there, Lord, let me sup with Thee, and Thou with me.

BENEVENTO. 7s. Double.

S. WEBBE.

1. While with ceaseless course the sun Hast-ed thro' the for-mer year,

FINE.

Man-y souls their race have run, Never more to meet us here;

D.S. We a lit-tle long-er wait, But how lit-tle none can know.

D. S.

Fix'd in their e-ter-nal state, They have done with all be-low;

2 As the winged arrow flies
  Speedily the mark to find ;
As the lightning from the skies
  Darts, and leaves no trace behind;
Swiftly thus our fleeting days
  Bear us down life's rapid stream;
Upward, Lord, our spirits raise;
  All below is but a dream.

3 Thanks for mercies past receive,
  Pardon of our sins renew;
Teach us henceforth how to live
  With eternity in view;
Bless Thy word to young and old,
  Fill us with a Saviour's love;
And when life's short tale is told,
  May we dwell with Thee above.

1. Be-fore Je - ho-vah's aw - ful throne, Ye nations t

Know that the Lord is God a - lone; He can cre - ate

2 His sovereign power, without our aid,
. Made us of clay, and formed us men;
And when, like wandering sheep, we
    strayed,
He brought us to His fold again.

3 We are His people, we His care,
Our souls and all our mortal frame:
What lasting honors shall we rear,
Almighty Maker, to Thy name.

4 We'll crowd Thy gates with thank-
    ful songs,
High as the heavens our voices raise:
And earth, with her ten thousand
    tongues,   [praise.
Shall fill their courts with sounding

5 Wide as the world is Thy command,
Vast as eternity Thy love;
Firm as a rock Thy truth must stand,
When rolling years shall cease to
    move.   ——

1 From all that dwell below the skies,
Let the Creator's praise arise:
Let the Redeemer's name be sung
Through every land, by every tongue.

2 Eternal are Thy mercies, Lord;
Eternal truth attends Thy word;
Thy praise shall sound from shore to
    shore,
Till suns shall set and rise no more.

1 My God, in wh
Of boundless
    known,
Hide me beneath
Till the dark cl

2 Up to the heav
The Lord will n
He sends His ang
And saves me f
    storm.

3 Be Thou exalte
Above the he
Thy power on ea
And land to lan
    ——

1 Dismiss us with
Help us to feed
All that has been
And let Thy tr

2 Though we are
. Wash all our w
Give every fetter
And bid us all

    Dox

Praise God, from
    flow;
Praise Him, all cr
Praise Him above
Praise Father, Sor

1. How te-dious and tasteless the hours, When Jesus no long-er I see!
Sweet prospects, sweet birds, and sweet flow'rs, Have lost all their sweetness with me;

D.C. *But when I am hap-py in Him, De-cem-ber's as pleas-ant as May.*

The mid-sum-mer sun shines but dim, The fields strive in vain to look gay;

2 His name yields the richest perfume,
And sweeter than music His voice;
His presence disperses my gloom,
And makes all within me rejoice:
I should, were He always thus nigh,
Have nothing to wish or to fear;
No mortal so happy as I,
My summer would last all the year.

3 Content with beholding His face,
My all to His pleasure resigned,
No changes of season or place
Would make any change in my mind.
While bless'd with a sense of His love,
A palace a toy would appear;
And prisons would palaces prove,
If Jesus would dwell with me there.

4 Dear Lord, if indeed I am Thine,
If Thou art my sun and my song,
Say, why do I languish and pine,
And why are my winters so long?
Oh, drive these dark clouds from my sky,
Thy soul-cheering presence restore;
Or take me unto Thee on high,
Where winter and clouds are no more.

1 Ye angels who stand round the throne,
And view my Immanuel's face,
In rapturous songs make Him known;
Tune, tune your soft harps to His praise.
He formed you the spirits you are,
So happy, so noble, so good;
While others sunk down in despair,
Confirmed by His power, ye stood.

2 Ye saints who stand nearer than they,
And cast your bright crowns at His feet,
His grace and His glory display,
And all His rich mercy repeat:
He snatched you from hell and the grave,
He ransom'd from death and despair,
For you He was mighty to save,
Almighty to bring you safe there.

3 Oh, when will the period appear,
When I shall unite in your song?
I'm weary of lingering here,
And I to your Saviour belong.
I'm fettered and chained up in clay;
I struggle and pant to be free;
I long to be soaring away,
My God and my Saviour to see.

D. W. MILLER.

1. Out of the dark-ness and in - to the light, Out of the
2. Safe, through the val - ley and shad-ow of death, Safe, at the

fan-cy in - to the sight, Out of the sor-row in - to the joy,
noon-day from pest'lent breath; Safe, tho' a thousand fall at our side,

In - to the glo - ry which knows not alloy; Thus wilt Thou lead us,
Safe, when most sorely and fiercely we're tried; Thus wilt Thou keep us,

Fa-ther a - bove, By the strong hand of Thy mer - ci-ful love.
Pa - rent of good, Fit-ted to en - ter Thy shin - ing a-bode.

3 Home to the city whose builder is God,
Home to the angels' bright, blessed abode;
Home where the cherub and seraphim greet,
Home where the saintly and purified meet;
Thus wilt Thou bring us, Jesus, our Lord,
E'en to that Presence our hearts have adored.

D. W. MILLER.

1. Swell the an - them, raise the song, Prais - es to our God be - long;

D. C. *Swell the an - them, raise the song, Prais - es to our God be - long;*

Saints and an - gels, join to sing Praise to heav'n's almight-y King.

FINE.

Saints and an - gels, join to sing Praise to heav'n's almight - y King.

SOLO.

Bless-ings from His lib - 'ral hand Pour around this hap-py land;

D. C.

Let our hearts, be-neath its sway, Hail the bright, tri-umph-ant day.

2 Now to Thee our joys ascend,
  Thou hast been our heavenly Friend:
  Guarded by Thy mighty power,
  Peace and freedom bless our shore.
Solo. Hark! the voice of nature sings
  Praises to the King of kings;
  Let us join the choral song,
  And the heavenly notes prolong.
Cho. Swell the anthem, raise the song. etc.

TRIUMPH. L. M.

D. W. MILLER.

Stand up, my soul, shake off thy fears, And gird the gos-pel ar - mor on;

March to the gates of end - less joy, Where Je-sus thy great Captain's gone.

1 Stand up, my soul, shake off thy fears,
  And gird the gospel armor on;
March to the gates of endless joy,
  Where Jesus thy great Captain's gone.

2 Hell and thy sins resist thy course,
  But hell and sins are vanquish'd foes;
Thy Jesus nailed them to the cross,
  And sung the triumph when He rose.

3 What tho' the prince of darkness rage,
  And waste the fury of his spite;
Eternal chains confine him down
  To fiery deeps and endless night.

4 What though thy inward lusts rebel;
  'Tis but a struggling gasp for life:
The weapons of victorious grace
  Shall slay thy sins and end the strife.

5 Then let my soul march boldly on,
  Press forward to the heavenly gate;
There peace and joy eternal reign,
  And glittering robes for conquerors
    wait.

1 Lord, I am Thine, entirely Thine,
Purchased and saved by blood divine;
With full consent Thine I would be,
And own Thy sovereign right in me.

2 Grant one poor sinner more a place
Among the children of Thy grace;
A wretched sinner, lost to God,
But ransom'd by Immanuel's blood.

3 Thine would I live. Thine would I die,
Be Thine through all eternity;
The vow is past beyond repeal;
Now will I set the solemn seal.

4 Here at that cross where flows the
    blood
That bought my guilty soul for God;
Thee, my new Master, now I call,
I consecrate to Thee my all.

5 Do Thou assist a feeble worm,
The great engagement to perform;
Thy grace can full assistance lend;
And on that grace I dare depend.

GIARDINI.

Come, Thou al - might y King, Help us Thy name to

sing, Help us to praise. Fa - ther! all glo - ri - ous, O'er all vic-

to - ri - ous, Come, and reign o - ver us, An - cient of Days.

1 Come, Thou almighty King,
  Help us Thy name to sing,
    Help us to praise.
  Father! all glorious,
  O'er all victorious,
  Come, and reign over us,
    Ancient of Days.

2 Jesus, our Lord, arise,
  Scatter our enemies,
    And make them fall.
  Let Thine almighty aid
  Our sure defense be made;
  Our souls on Thee be staid;
    Lord, hear our call.

3 Come, Thou incarnate Word,
  Gird on Thy mighty sword;
    Our prayer attend.

  Come, and Thy people bless,
  And give Thy word success
  Spirit of holiness,
    On us descend.

4 Come, Holy Comforter,
  Thy sacred witness bear
    In this glad hour.
  Thou, who almighty art,
  Now rule in every heart,
  And ne'er from us depart,
    Spirit of power.

5 To the great One in Three,
  The highest praises be
    Hence evermore.
  His sovereign majesty
  May we in glory see,
  And to eternity
    Love and adore.

BURT. C. M.

D. W. MILLER.

1. Thee we a - dore, eternal Name, And humbly own to Thee, How feeble

2. The year rolls round and steals away The breath that first it gave; What e'er we

is our mor-tal frame, What dying worms are we, What dying worms are we!

do, where'er we be, We're trav'ling to the grave, We're trav'ling to the grave.

3 Great God, on what a slender thread
Hang everlasting things!
The eternal state of all the dead
Upon lifes feeble strings.

4 Waken, O Lord, our drowsy sense,
To walk this dang'rous road;
And if our souls be hurried hence,
May they be found with God.

HAVEN. C. M.

D. W. MILLER.

1. Now to the ha - ven of Thy breast, O Son of man, I fly; Be

2. Pro - tect me from the furious blast; My shield and shelter be: Hide

Thou my ref - uge and my rest, For oh, the storm is nigh.

me, my Sav-iour, till o'er-past The storm of sin I see.

3 As o'er a parched and weary land
A rock extends its shade.
So hide me, Saviour, with Thy hand,
And screen my naked head.

4 How swift to save me didst Thou move
In every trying hour;
O! still protect me with Thy love,
And shield me with Thy power.

ENGLISH.

1. { Rise, my soul, and stretch thy wings, Thy bet-ter por-tion trace;
{ Rise, from tran-si-to-ry things, Tow'rd heav'n, thy native place;

Sun, and moon, and stars de-cay; Time shall soon this earth re-move:

Rise, my soul, and haste a - way To seats prepared a - bove.

2 Rivers to the ocean run,
    Nor stay in all their course;
Fire, ascending, seeks the sun;
    Both speed them to their source:
So a soul that's born of God,
    Pants to view His glorious face,
Upward tends to His abode,
    To rest in His embrace.

3 Cease, ye pilgrims, cease to mourn;
    Press onward to the prize;
Soon our Saviour will return,
    Triumphant in the skies.
Yet a season, and, you know,
    Happy entrance will be given;
All our sorrows left below,
    And earth exchanged for heaven.

1. There is a fount-ain filled with blood, Drawn from Immanuel's veins;

And sinners, plunged beneath that flood, Lose all their guilt-y stains;

D. S. *And sin-ners, plunged be-neath that flood, Lose all their guilt-y stains.*

Lose all their guilt - y stains, Lose all their guilt-y stains;

2 The dying thief rejoiced to see
That fountain in his day;
And there may I, though vile as he,
Wash all my sins away.

3 Thou dying Lamb! Thy precious
Shall never lose its power, [blood
Till all the ransomed Church of God
Are saved, to sin no more.

4 When this poor, lisping, stamm'ring
Lies silent in the grave, [tongue
Then, in a nobler, sweeter, song
I'll sing Thy power to save.

1 Salvation! oh, the joyful sound!
'T is pleasure to our ears;
A sovereign balm for every wound,
A cordial for our fears.

2 Buried in sorrow and in sin,
At hell's dark gate we lay;
But we arise, by grace divine,
To see a heavenly day.

3 Salvation! Let the echo fly
The spacious earth around,
While all the armies of the sky
Conspire to raise the sound.

BRADBURY

1. Sweet hour of pray'r, sweet hour of pray'r, That calls me from a

world of care, And bids me at my Fa - ther's throne Make
And oft es - caped the tempt - er's snare, By

all my wants and wish - es known: In sea - sons of dis-
thy re - turn, Sweet hour of pray'r.

FINE.

D. S.

tress and grief My soul has oft - en found re - lief,

2 Sweet hour of prayer, sweet hour of prayer,
Thy wings shall my petition bear
To Him whose truth and faithfulness
Engage the waiting soul to bless:
And since He bids me seek His face,
Believe His word, and trust His grace,
I'll cast on Him my every care.
And wait for thee, sweet hour of prayer.

3 Sweet hour of prayer, sweet hour of prayer,
May I thy consolation share,
Till from Mount Pisgah's lofty height
I view my home and take my flight:
This robe of flesh I'll drop, and rise,
To seize the everlasting prize,
And shout, while passing through the air,
Farewall, farewell, sweet hour of prayer.

MY SUMMONS.

D. W. MILLER.

Slowly and Gently.

1. My summons may come in the morning, Or the deep peaceful slumber of
2. It may come while I'm working for others, Or lay-ing out plans for my-

night; It may come with a lin - gering warning, Or as
self; It may come when I'm laid, as a well-worn And

quick as a flash of sunlight; It may come while I'm thinking of
use - less old book, on the shelf; It may come when my life, full of

heav-en, It may come while my tho'ts are astray; While I'm sit-ting a-
sweetness, Would fain have it tar - ry a while; It may come when my

lone in my dwelling, Or meeting some friend by the way. But the
sorrow's completeness Makes me welcome the call with a smile. Tho' it

day or the hour when the bidding Comes to me, I nev-er can
fall in the gen - tlest of whispers, Or sound with a deep, startling

know;   And I pray,   at the call   of the Master
kneel,   I pray on - ly that I   may be read-y,

answer, "I'm ready to go."
answer, dear Lord, "It is well."   **CHORUS.**

But the day,   or th

INST.

bid-ding   Comes to   me I nev - er can k

pray, at the call of the Mas-ter,   I may answer, "I'm re

INDEX

(113)

120   INDEX.

www.ingramcontent.com/pod-product-compliance
Lightning Source LLC
Chambersburg PA
CBHW030626270326
41927CB00007B/1325